THIS BOOK BELONGS TO:

_____

_____

TEST COLOR PAGE

TEST YOUR COLOR SUPPLIES ON THIS SKULLS TO SEE HOW THEY REACT TO THE PAGE

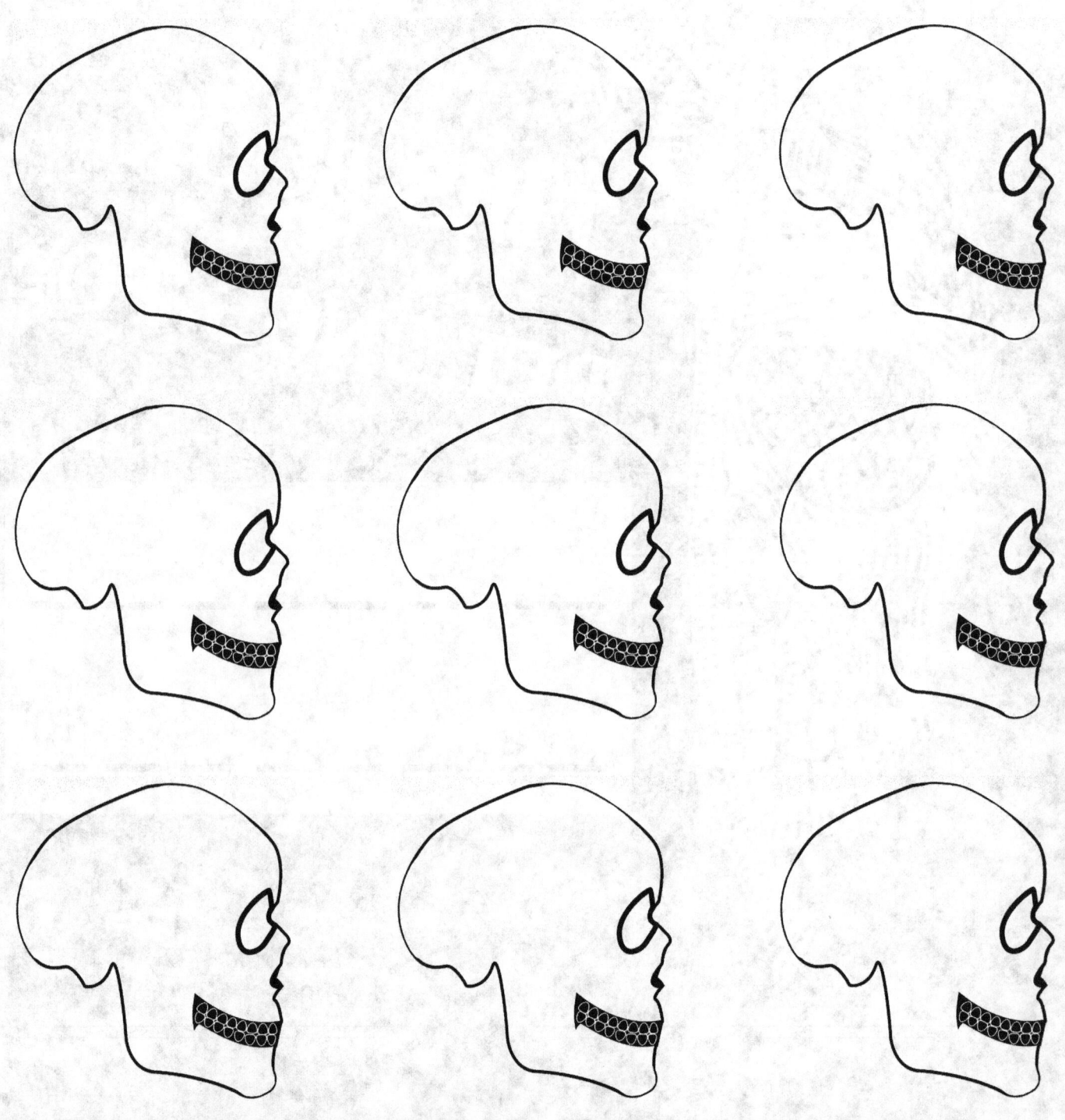

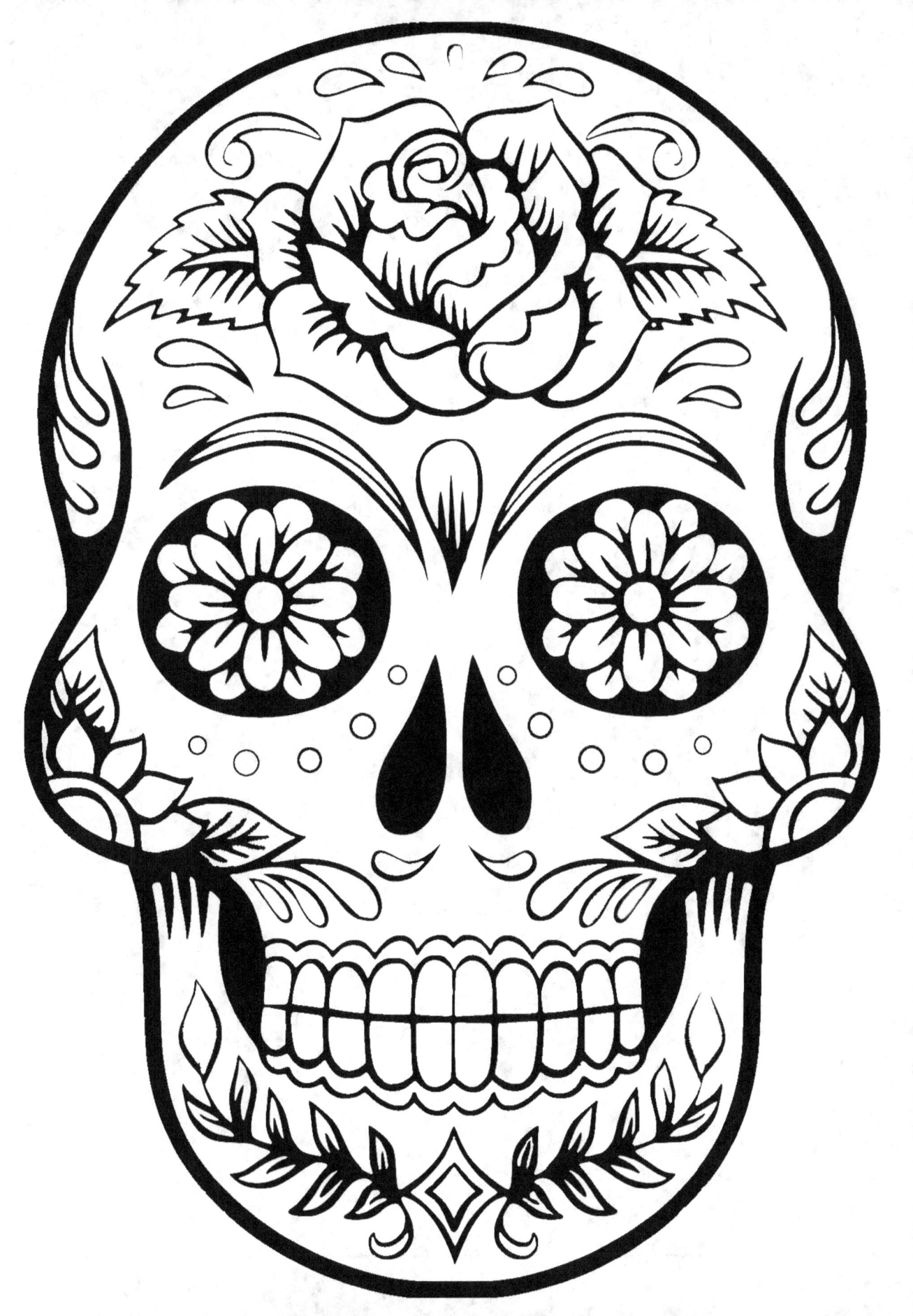

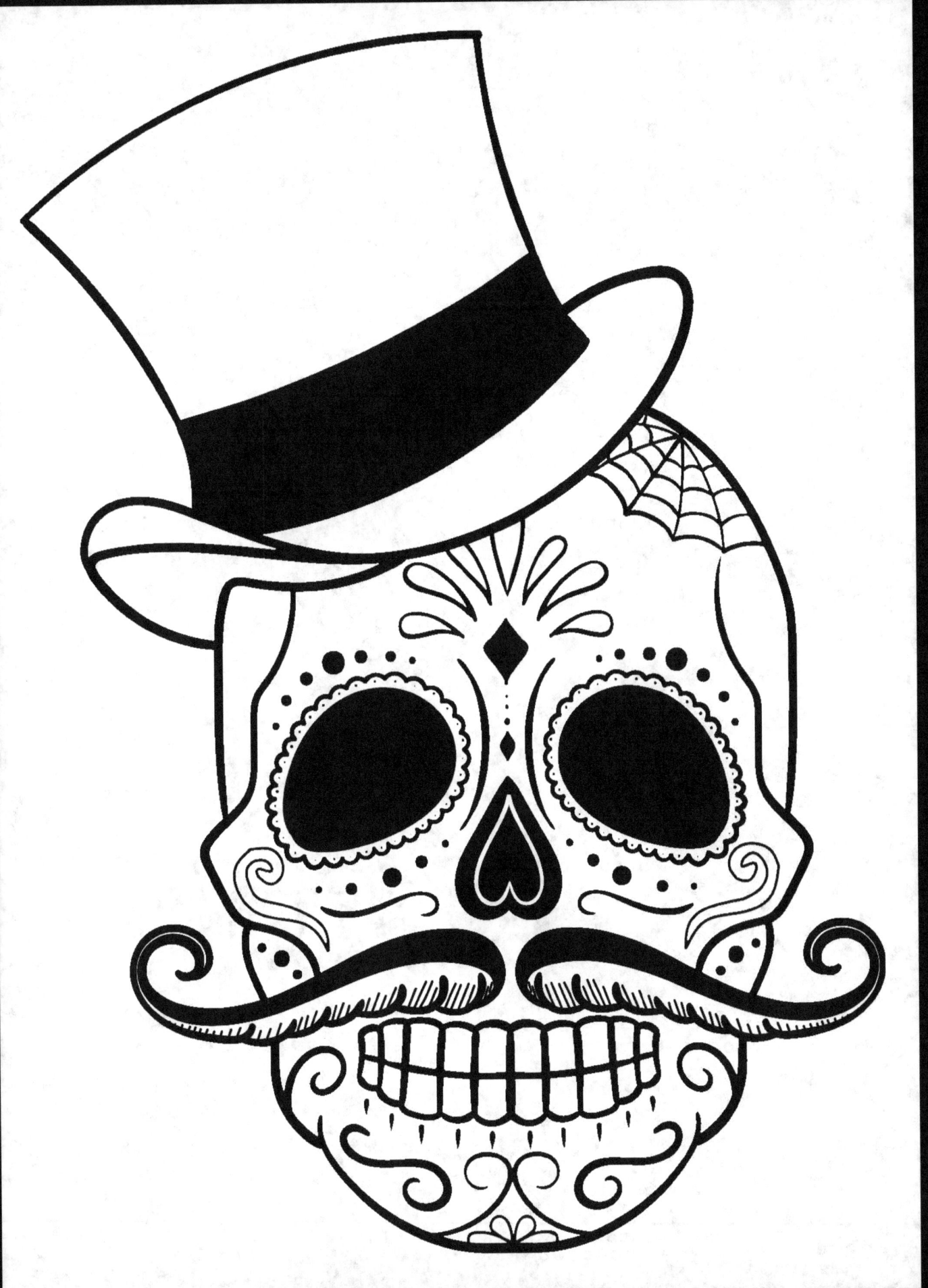

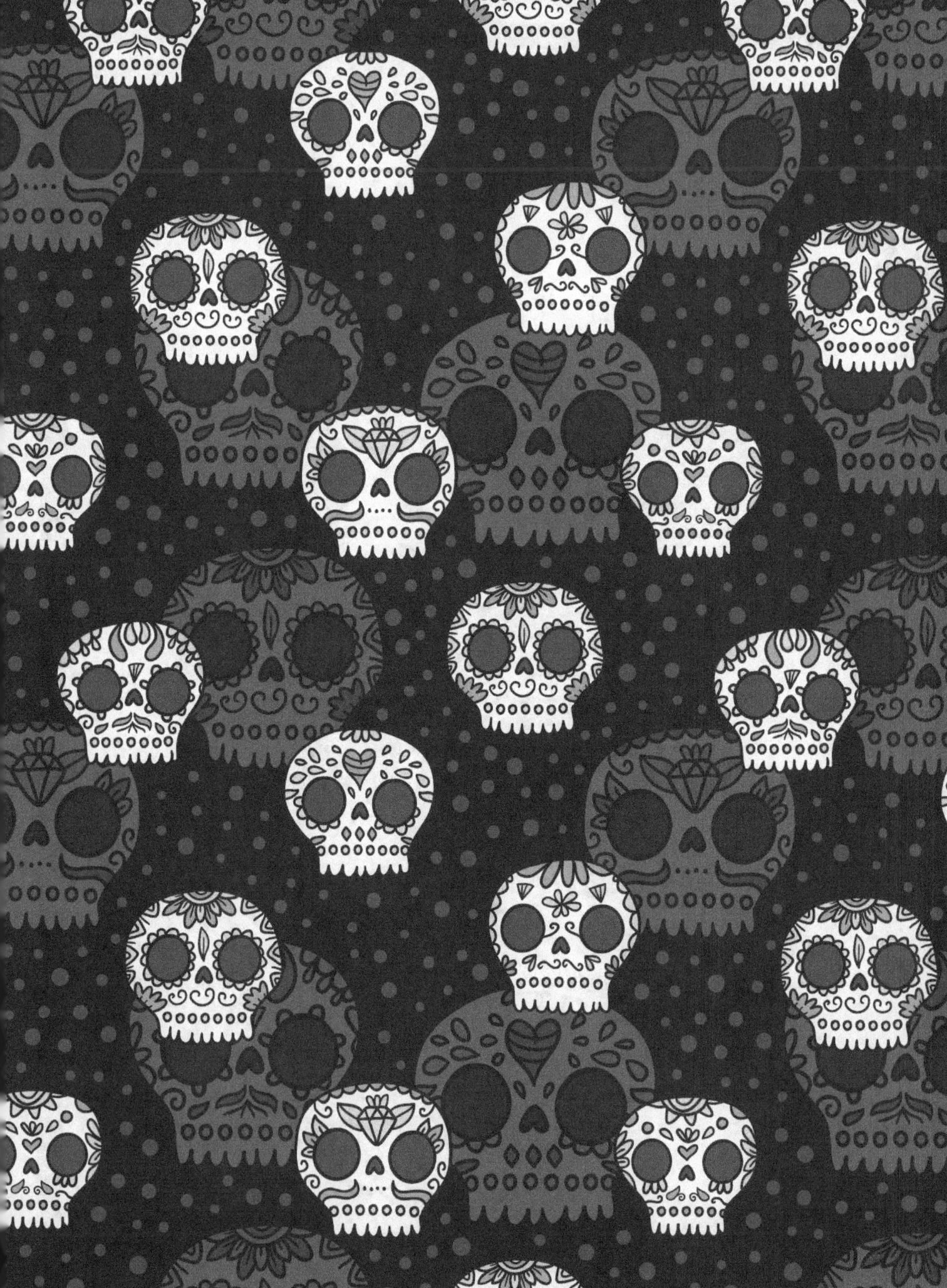

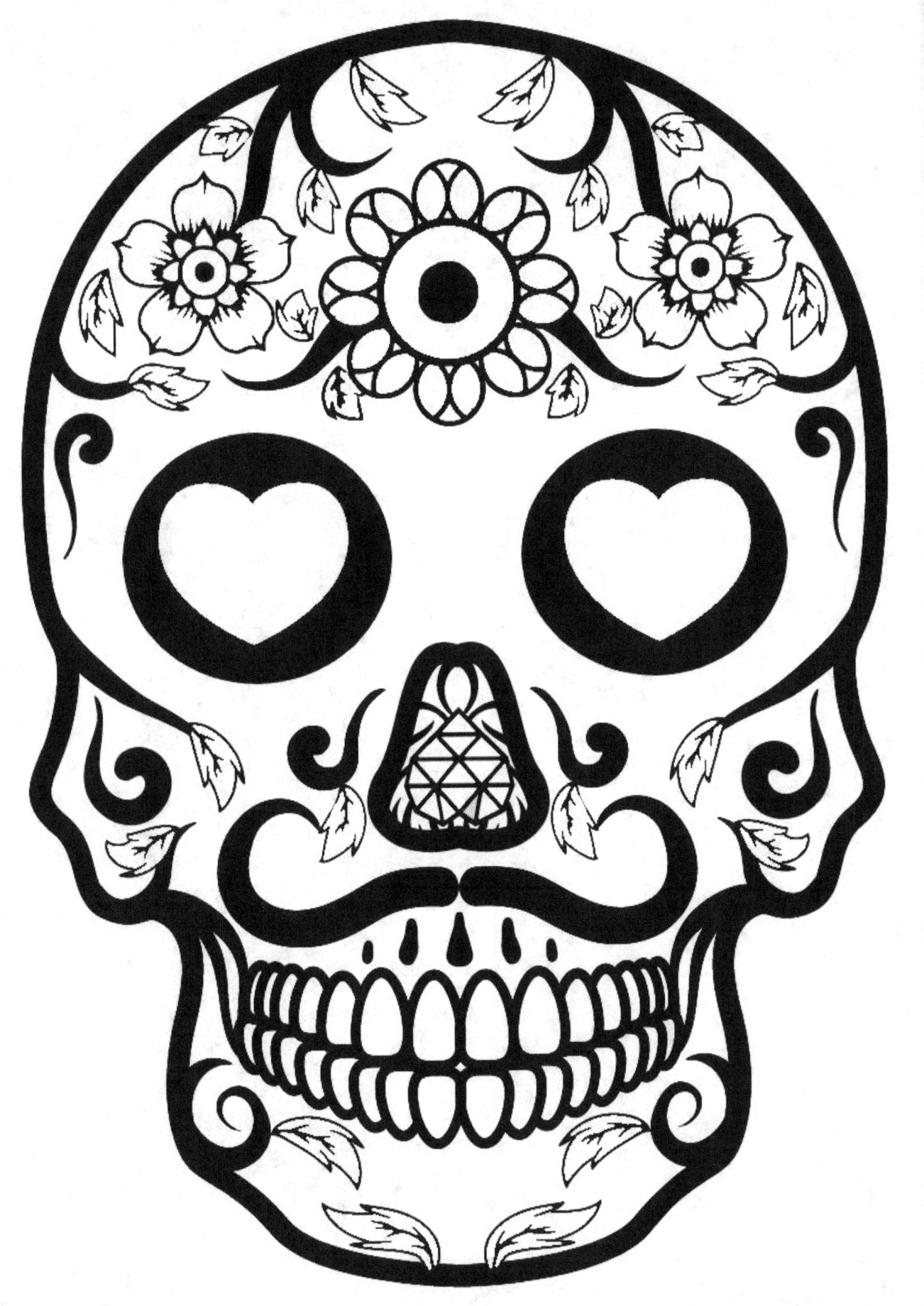

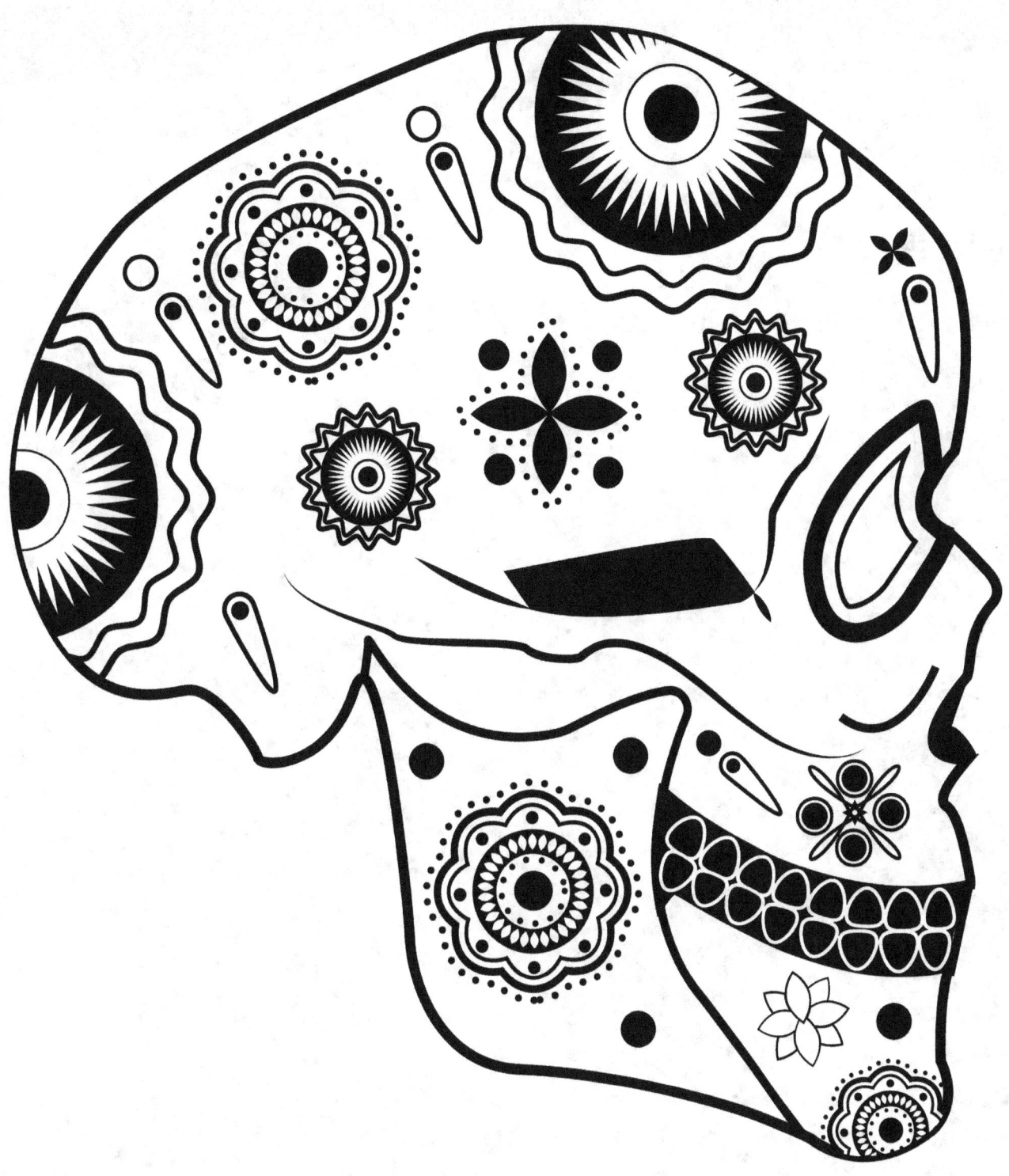

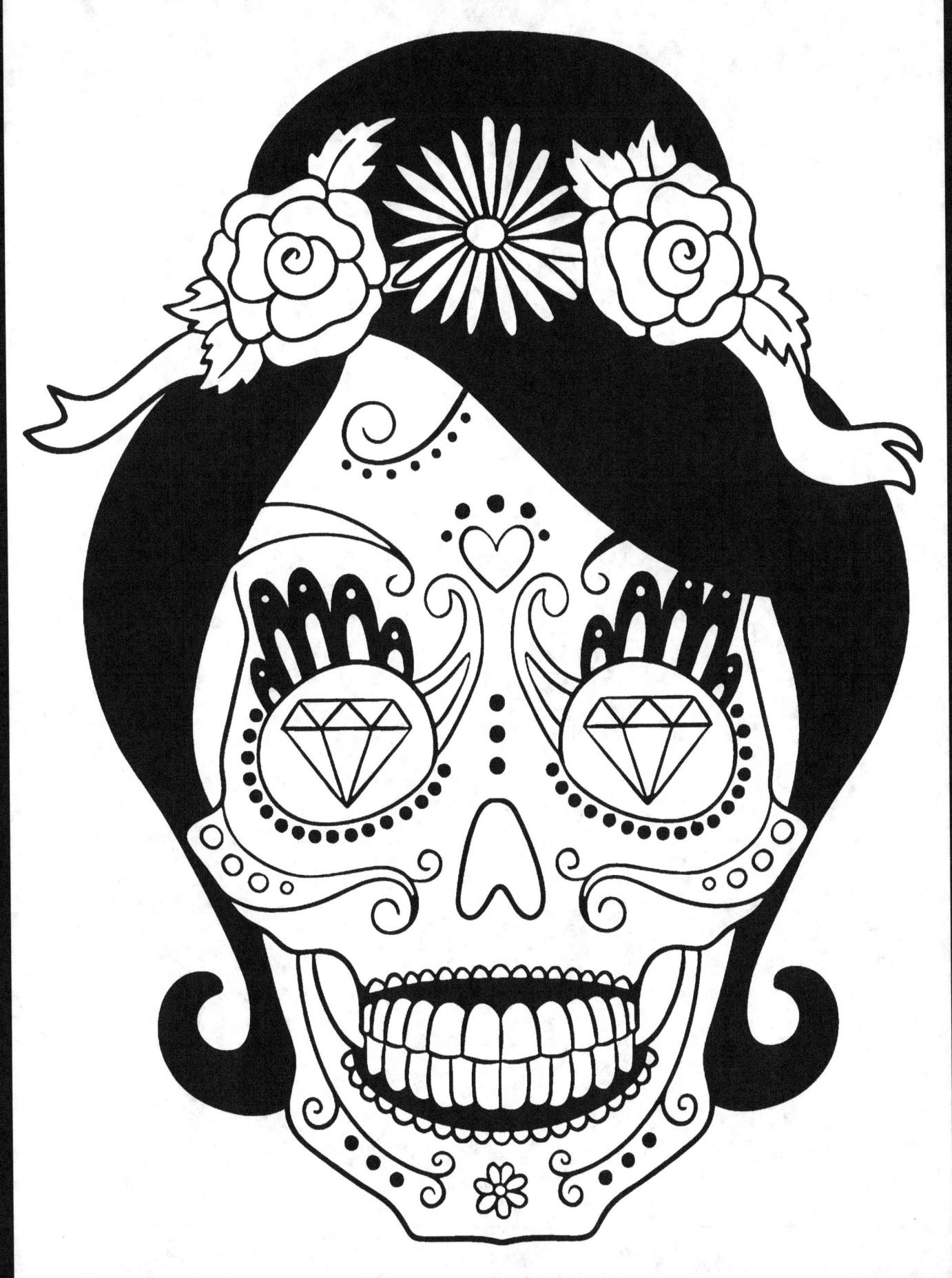

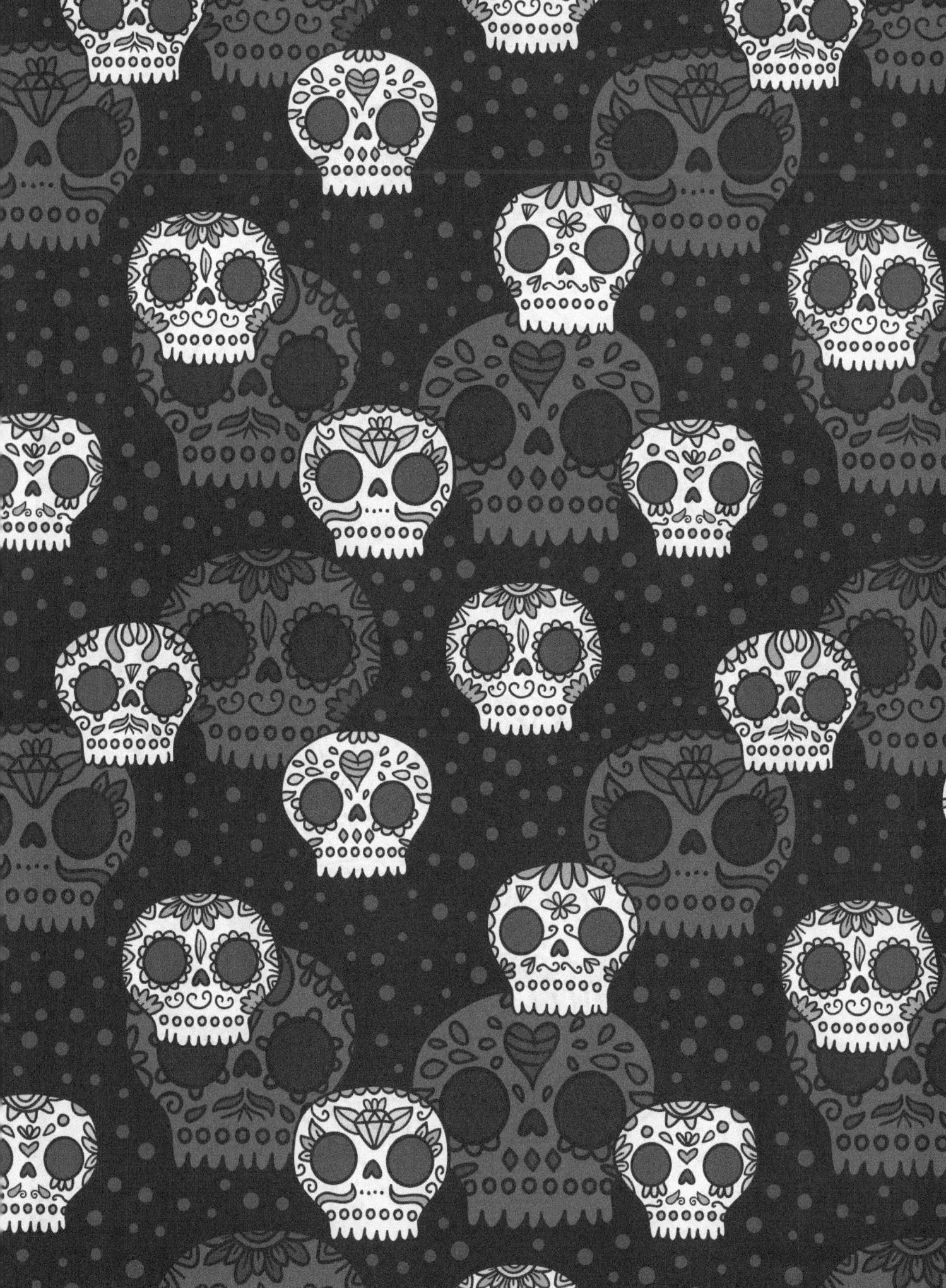

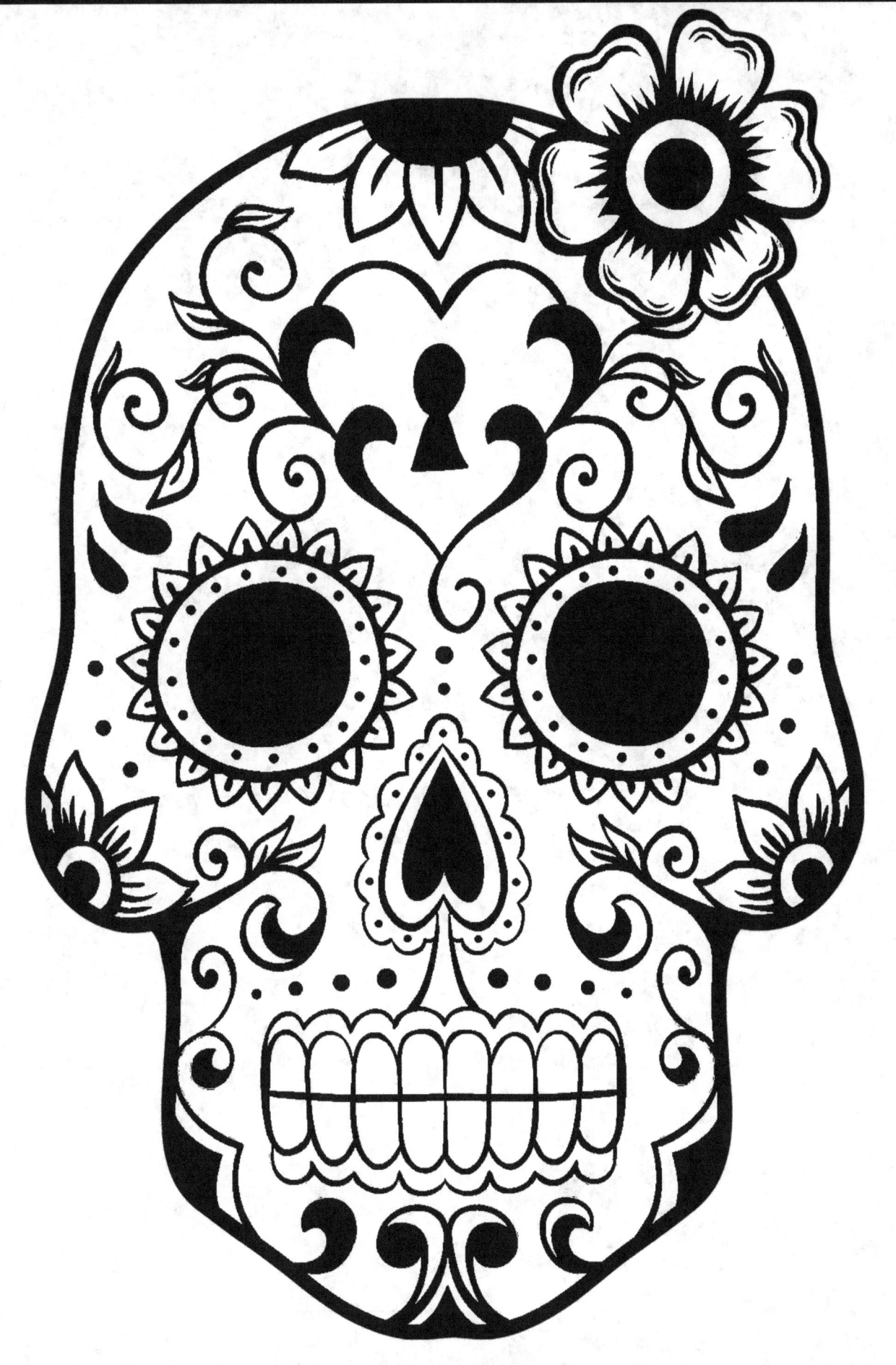

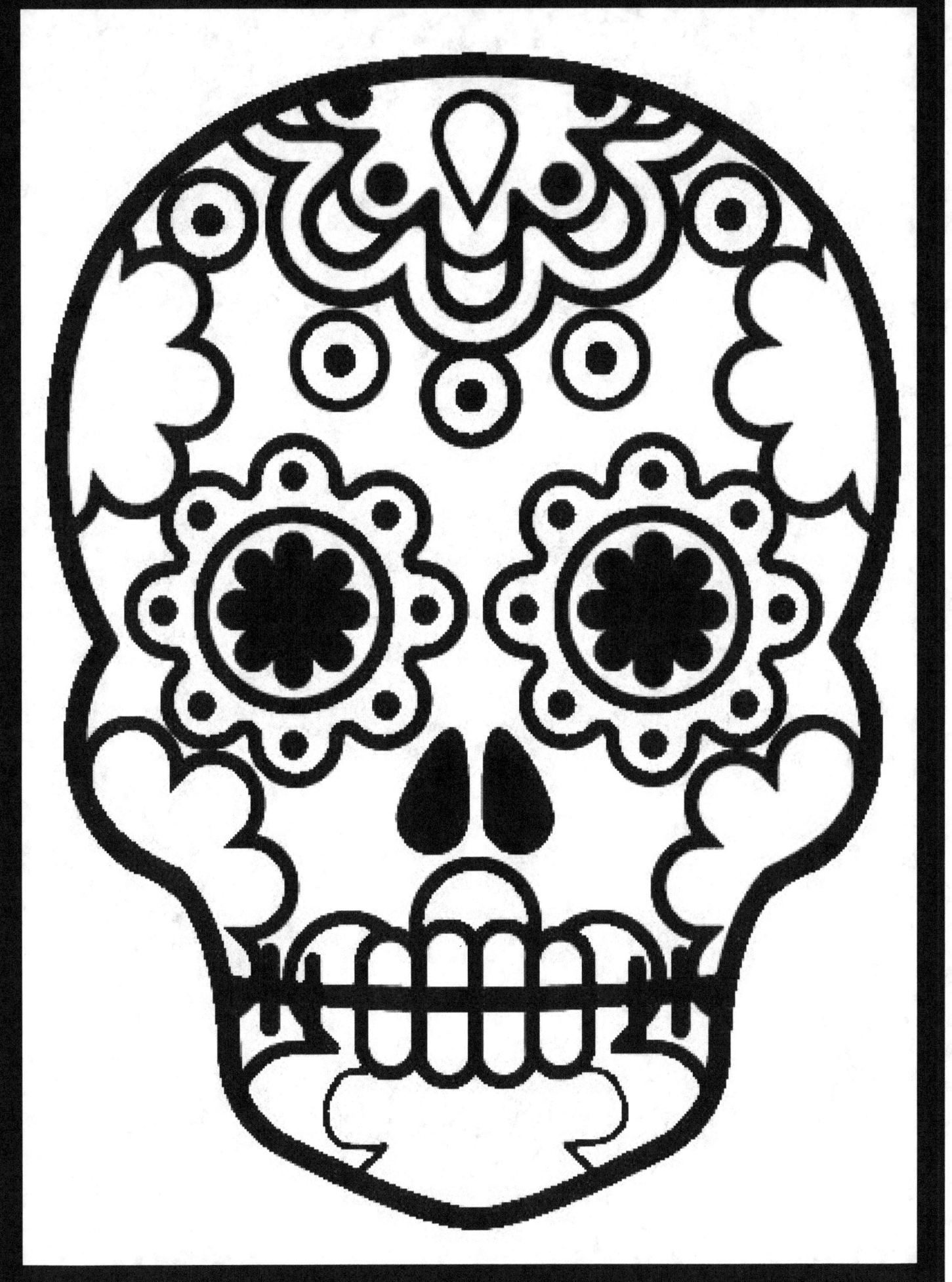

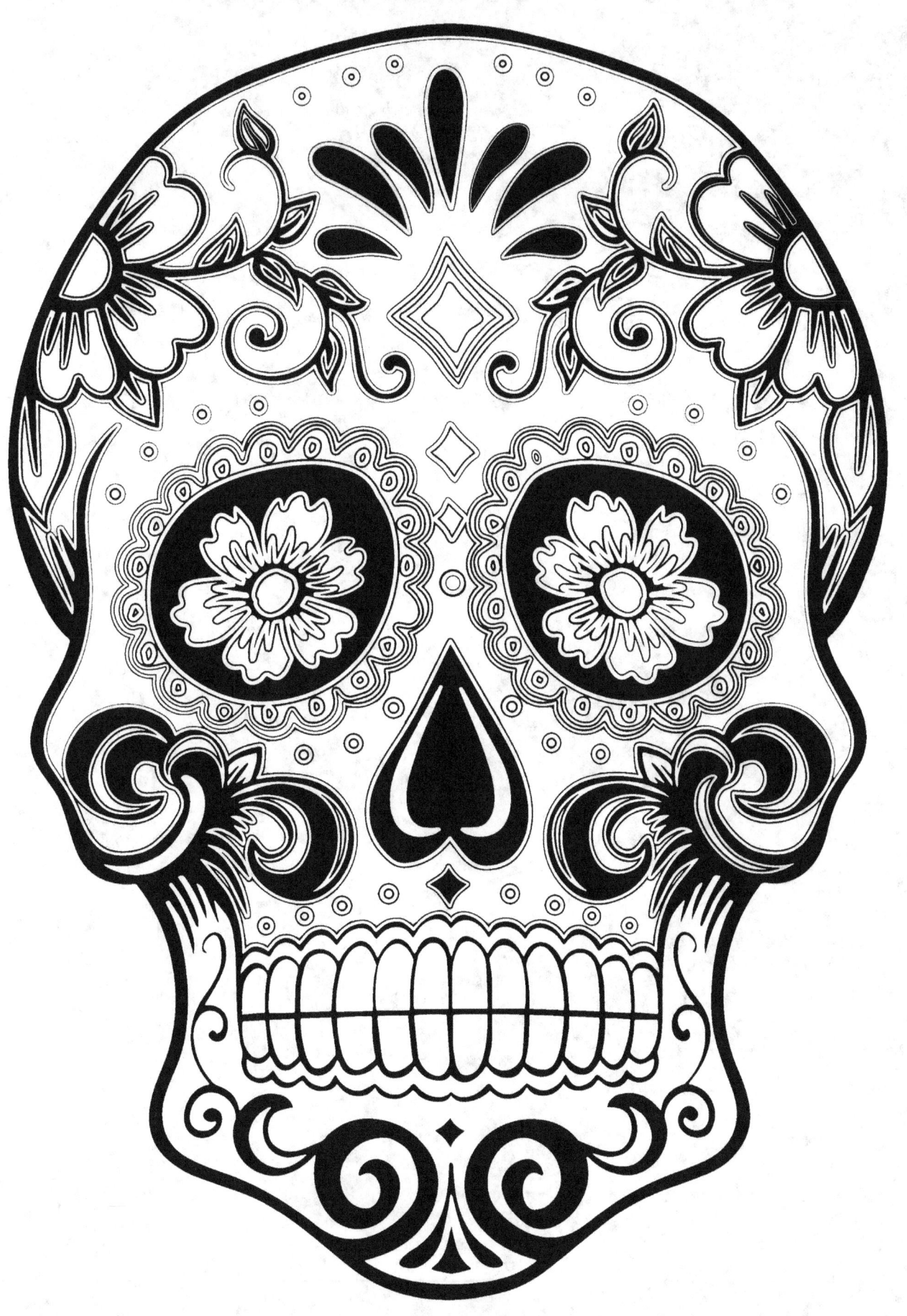

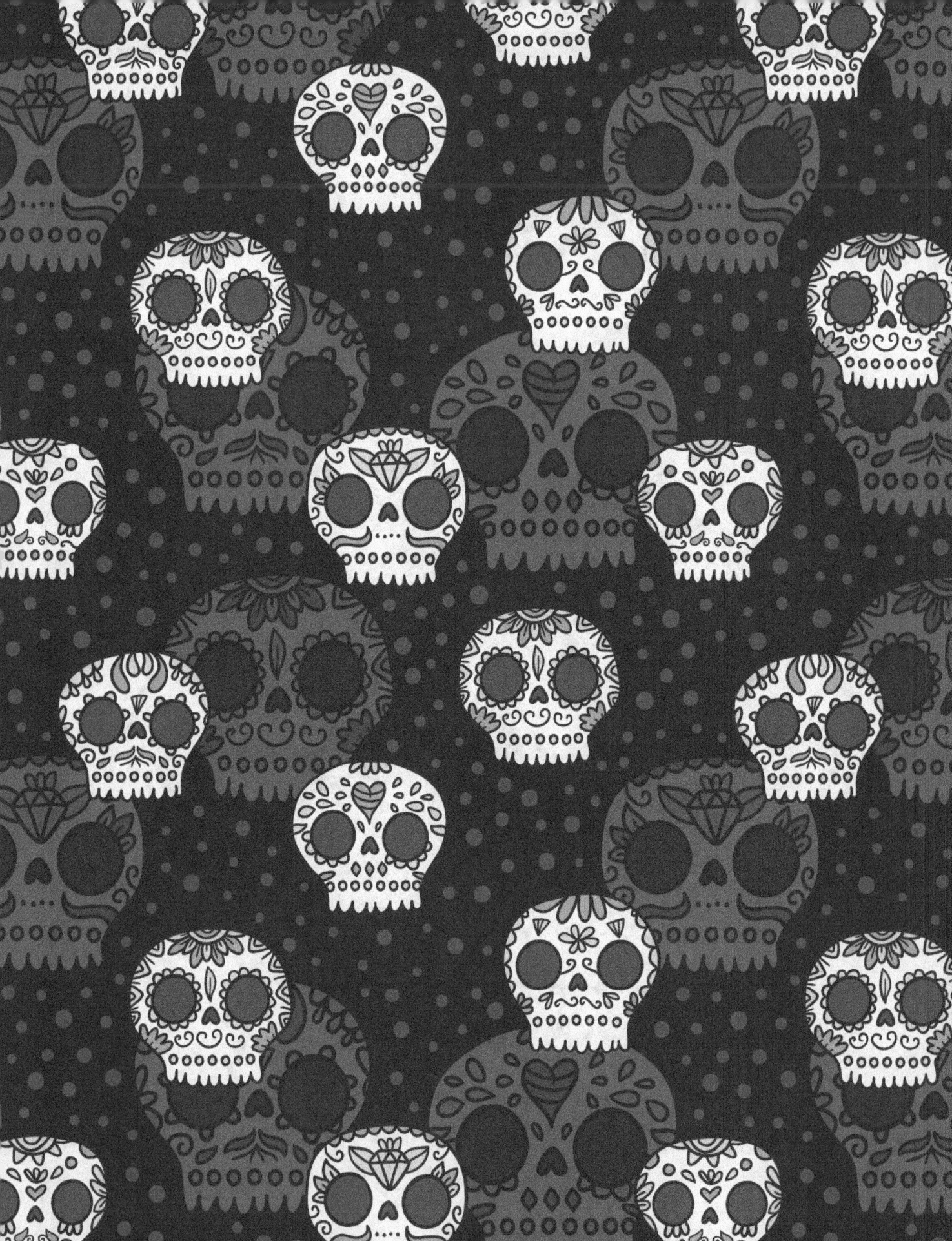

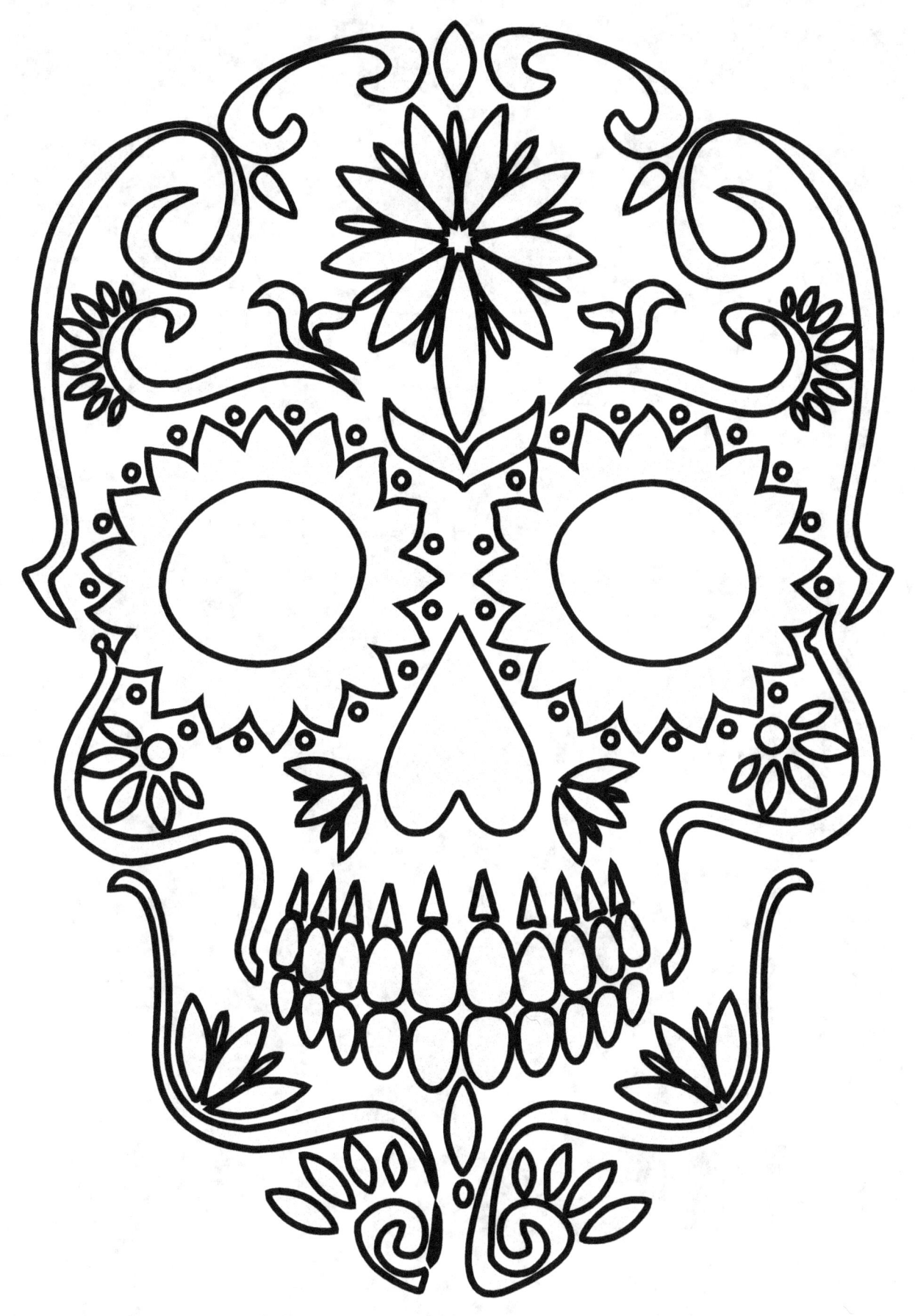

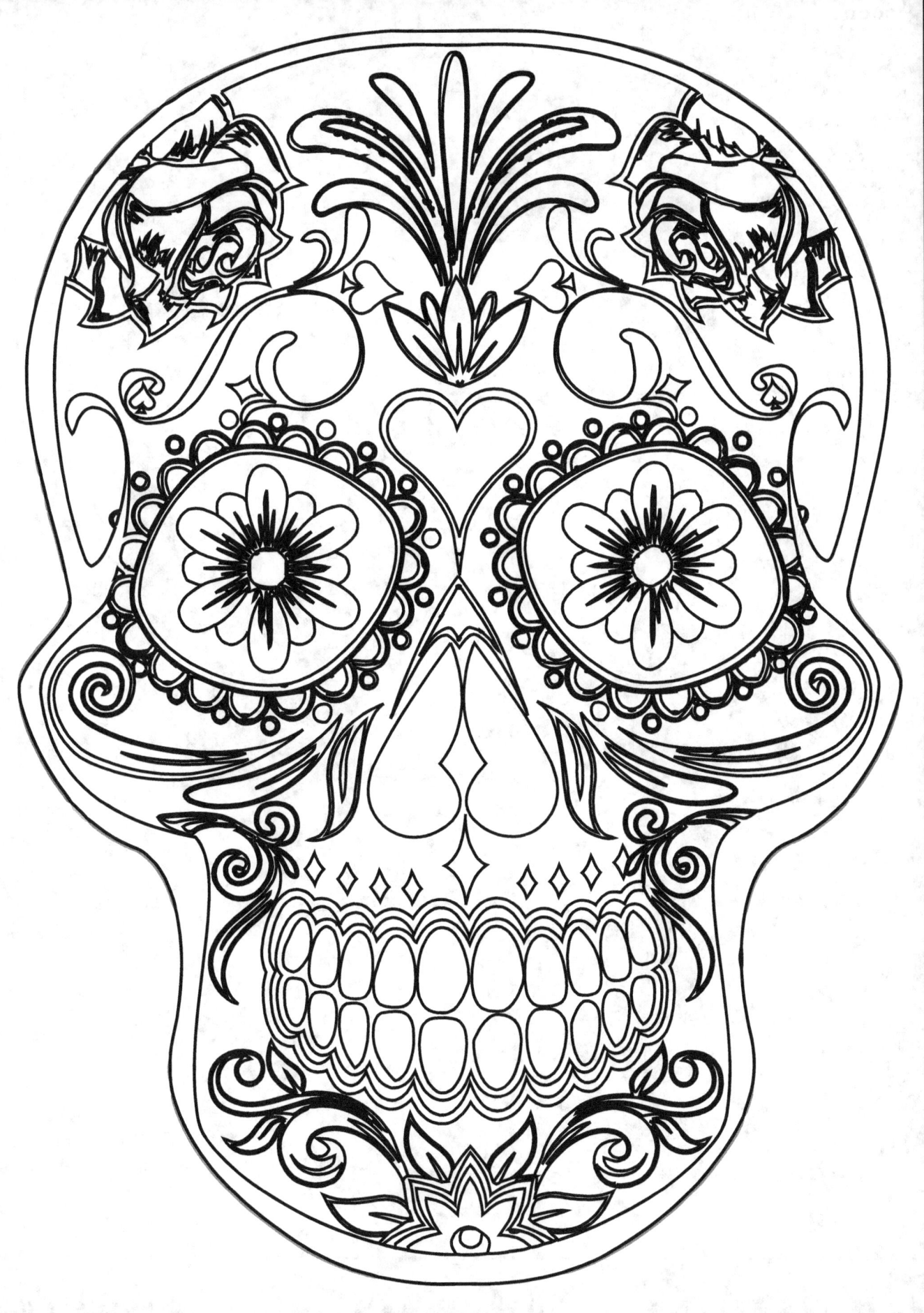

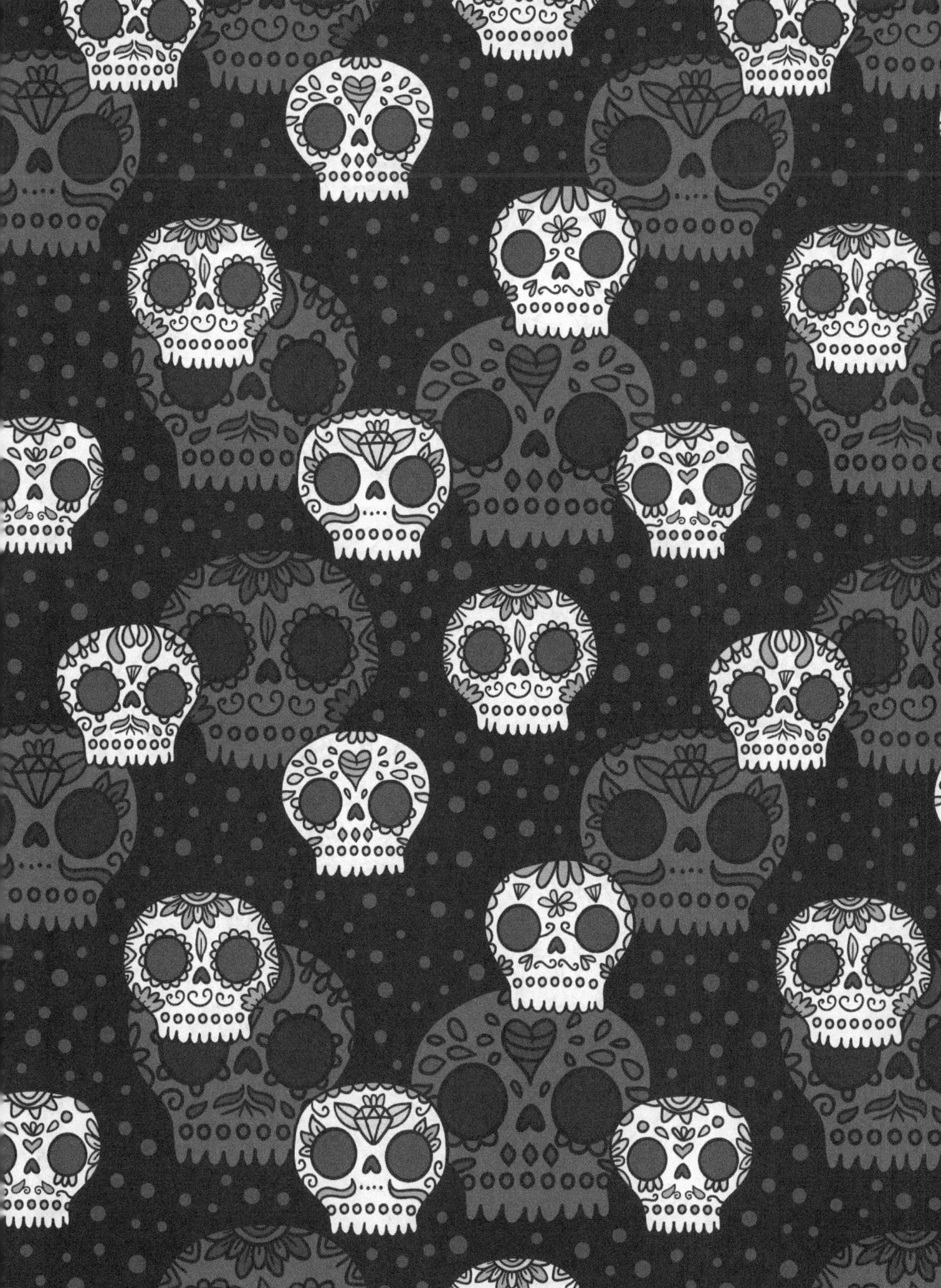

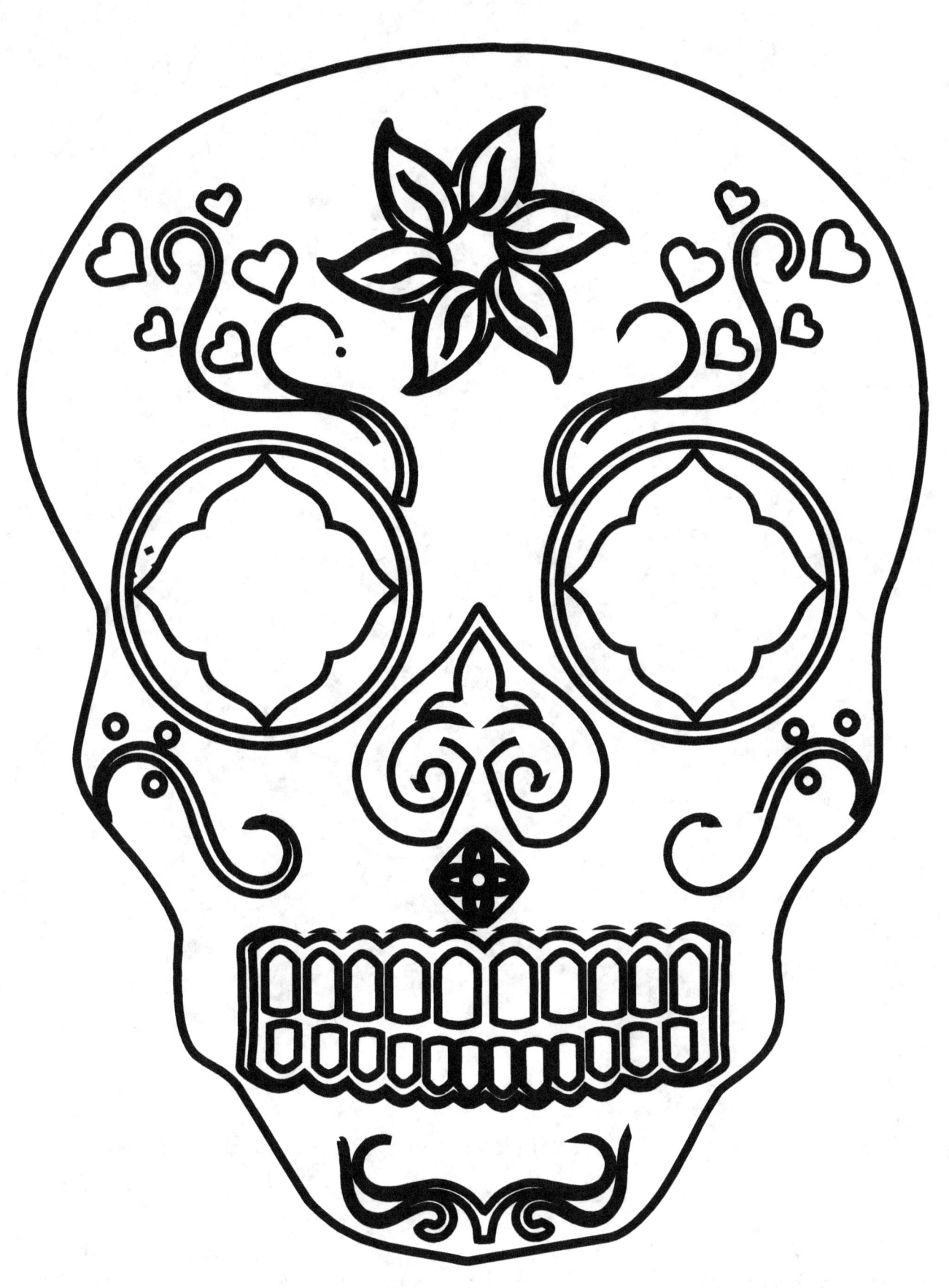

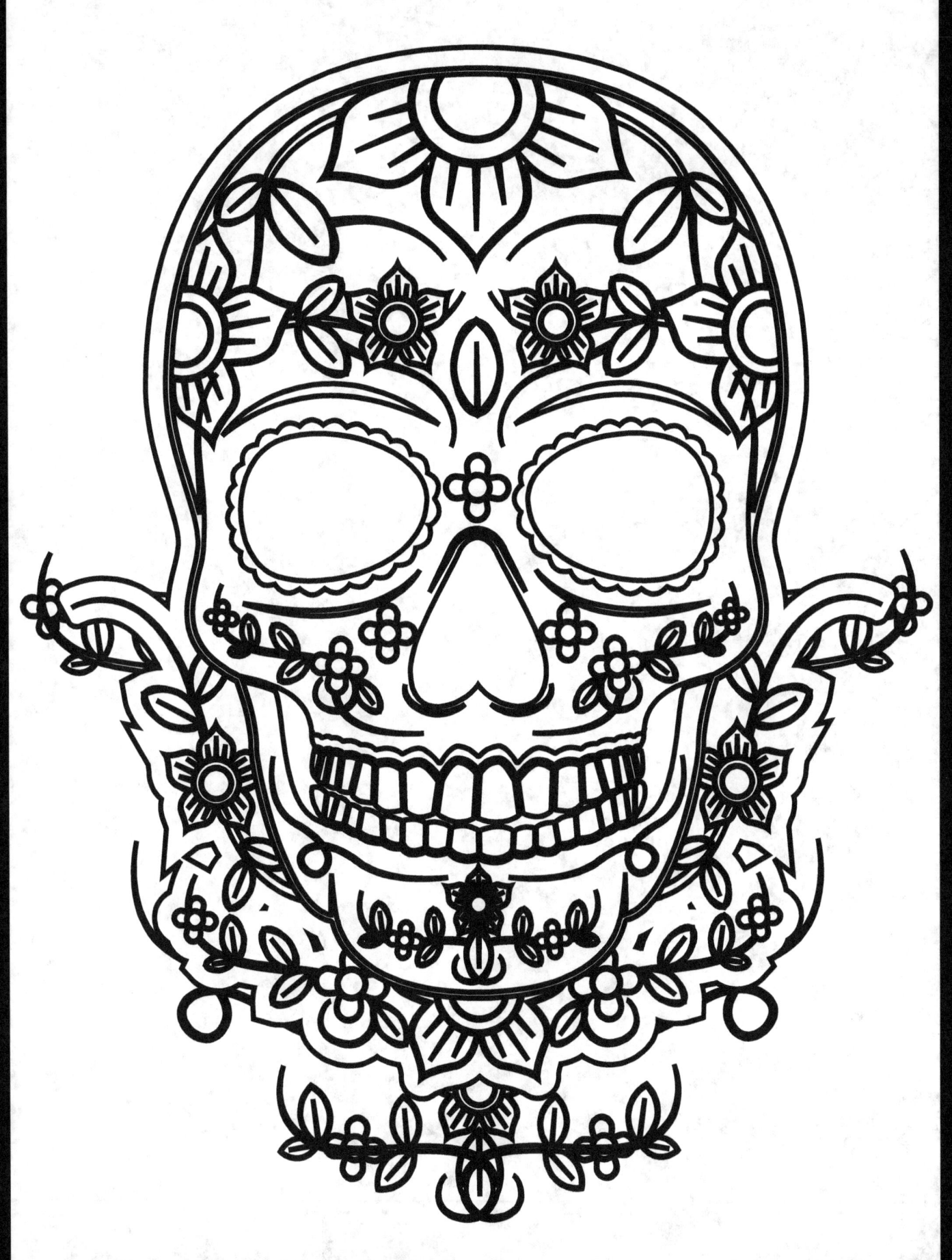

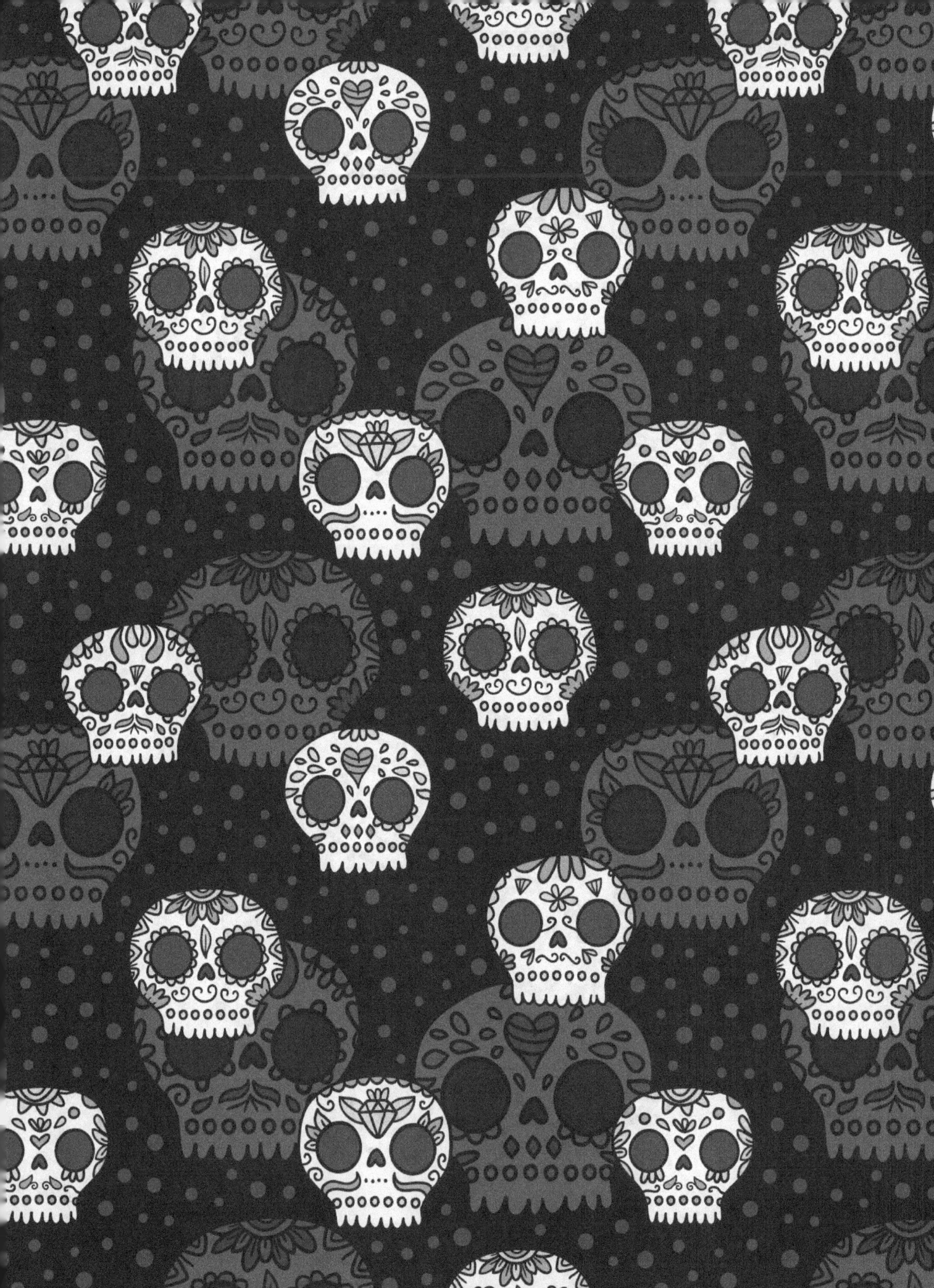

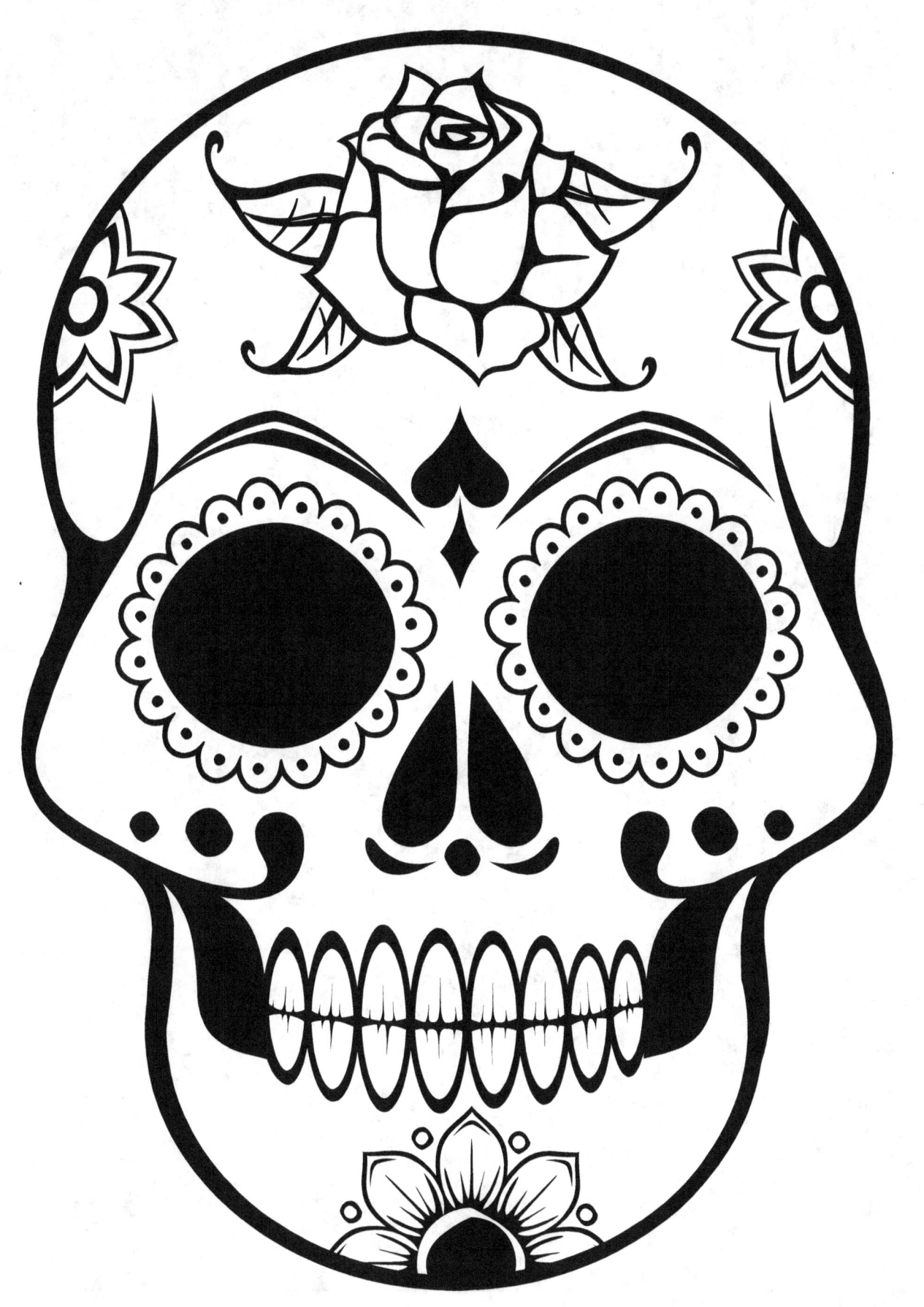

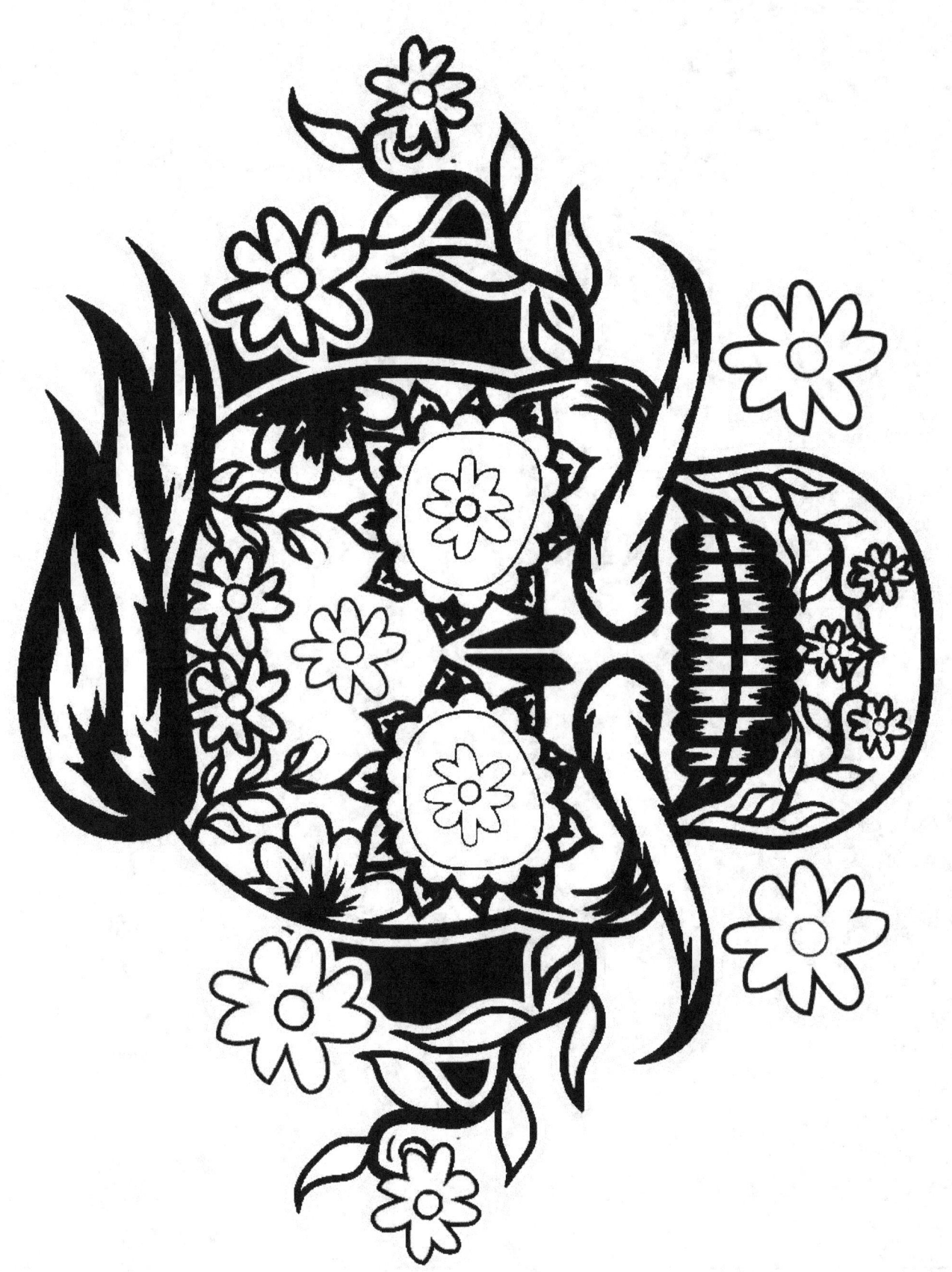

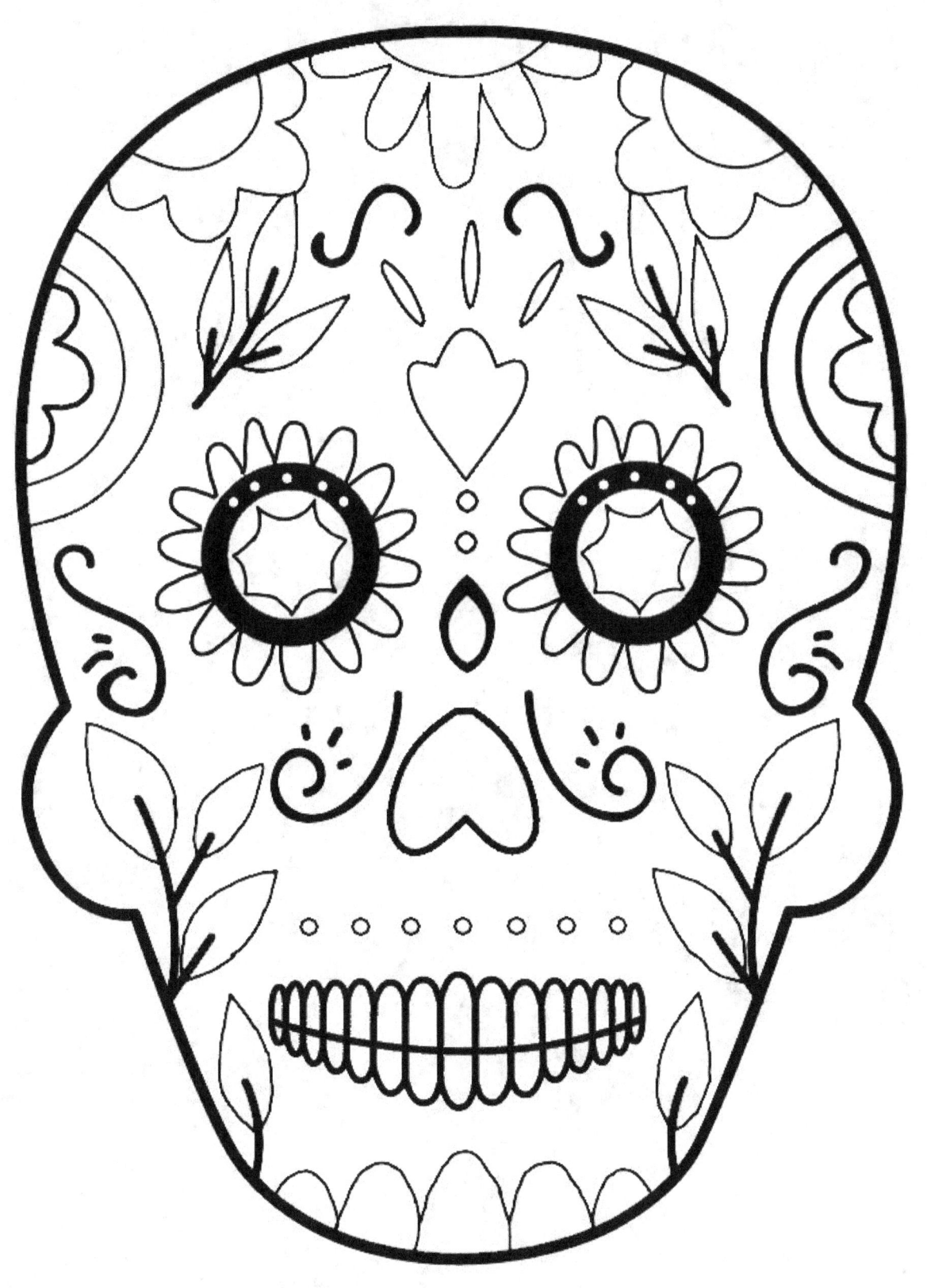

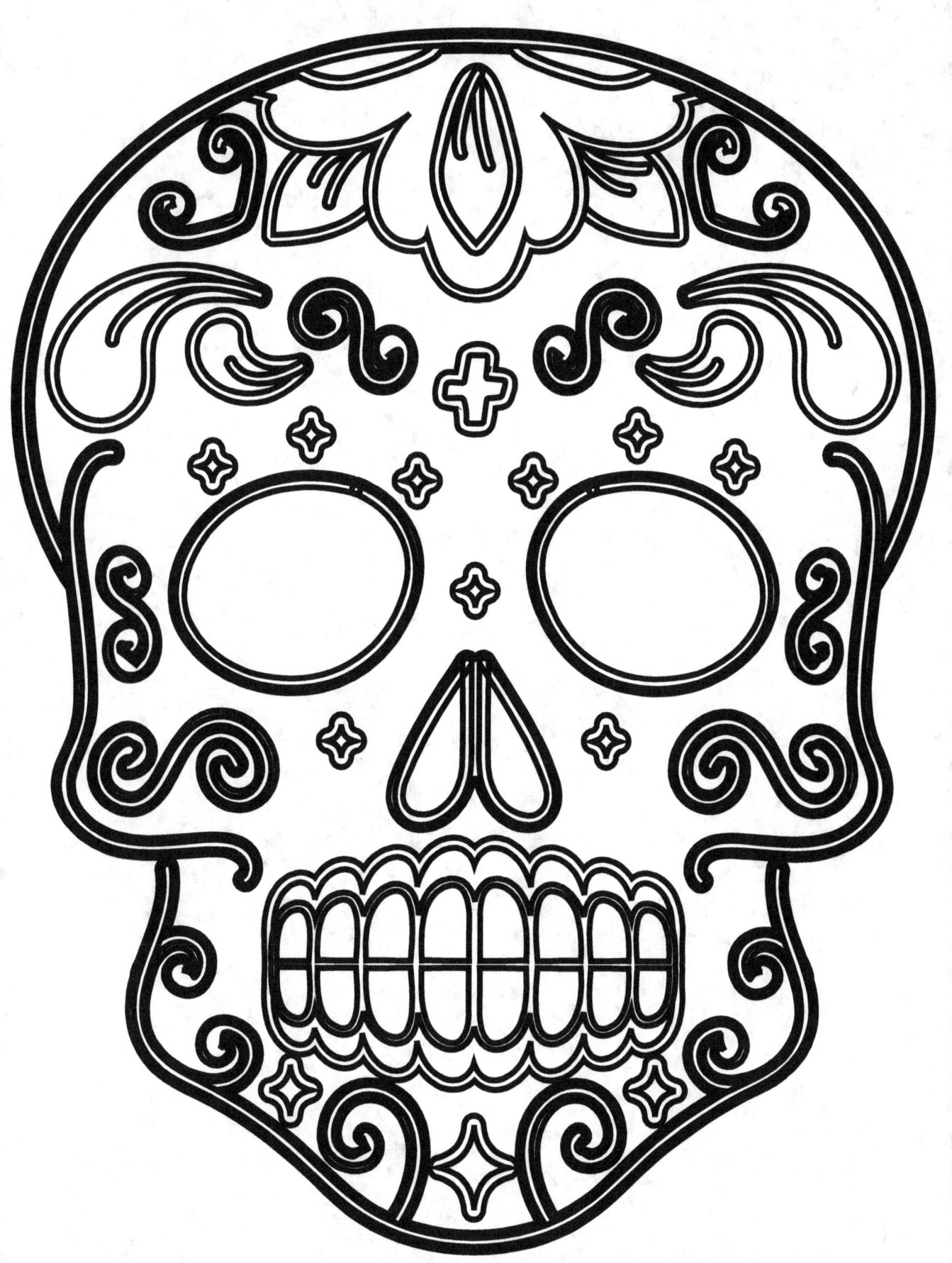

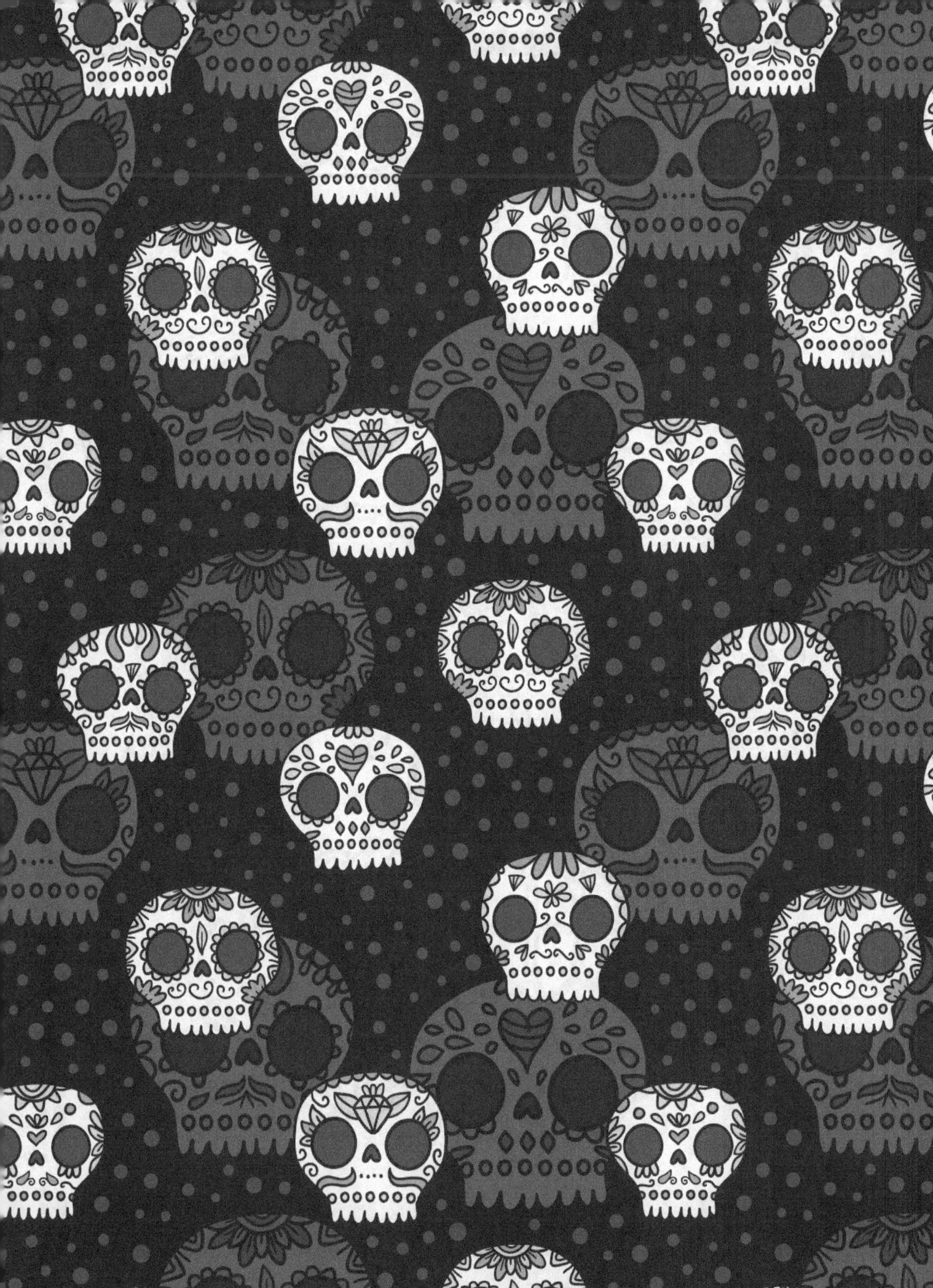

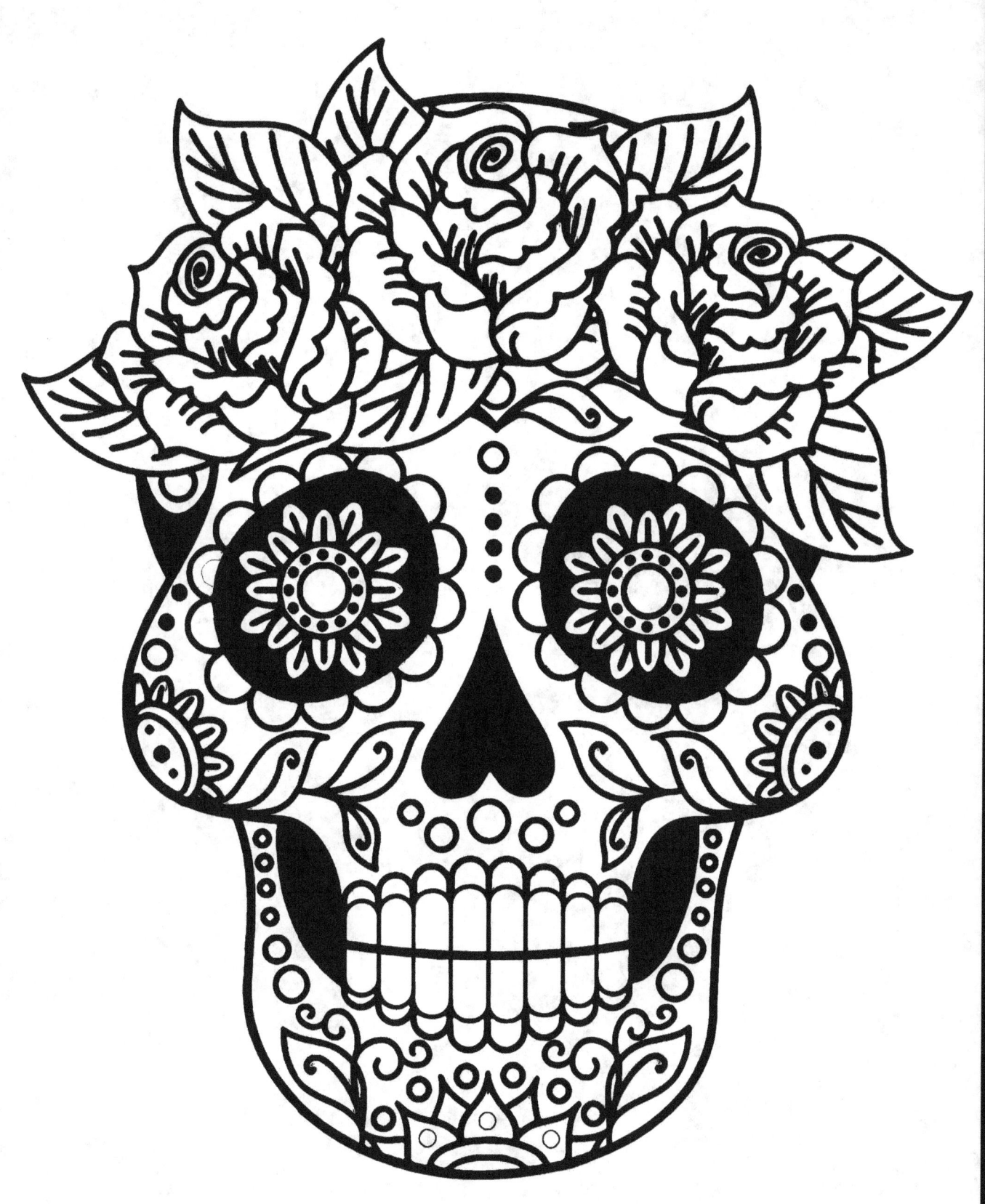

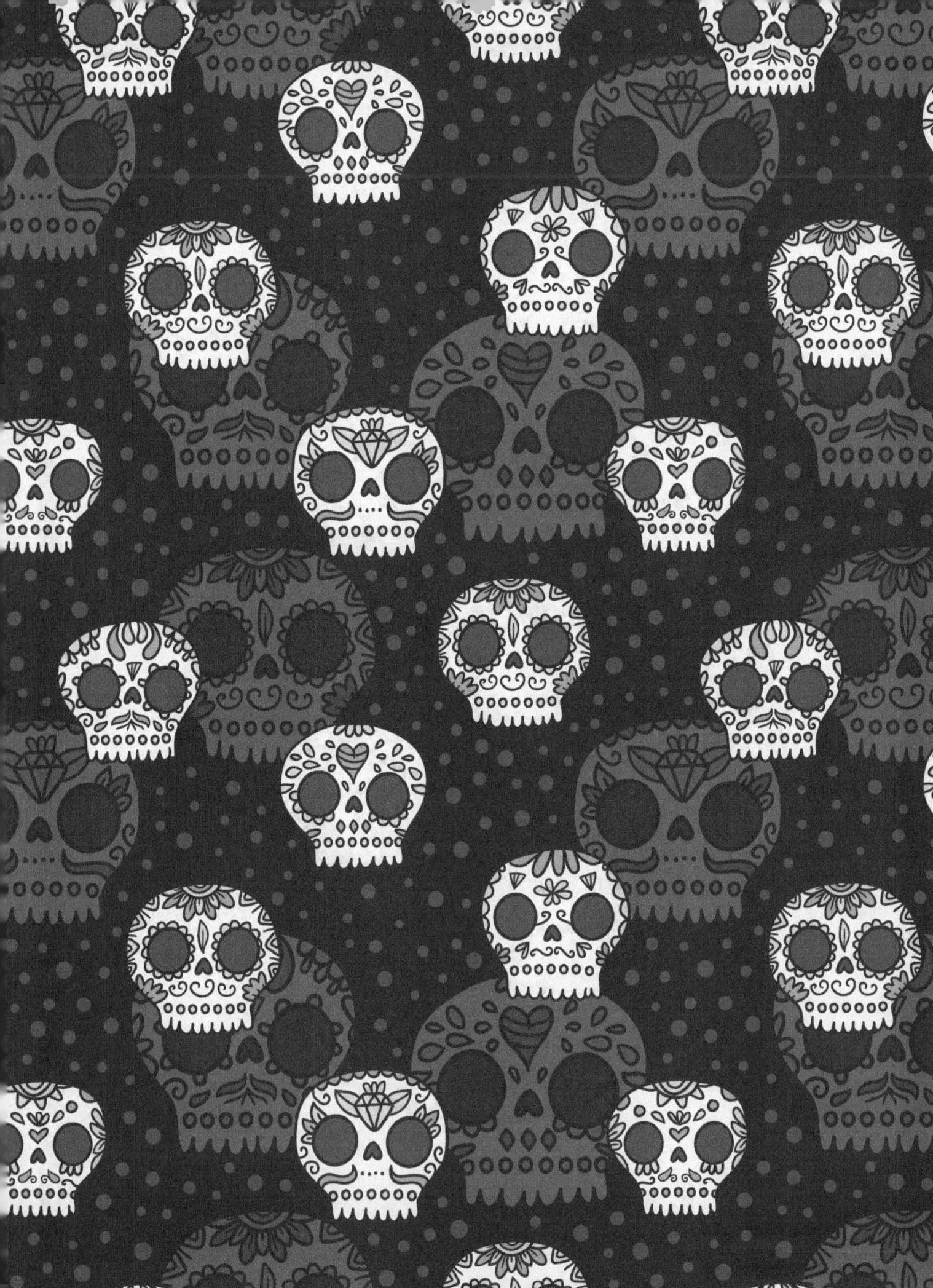

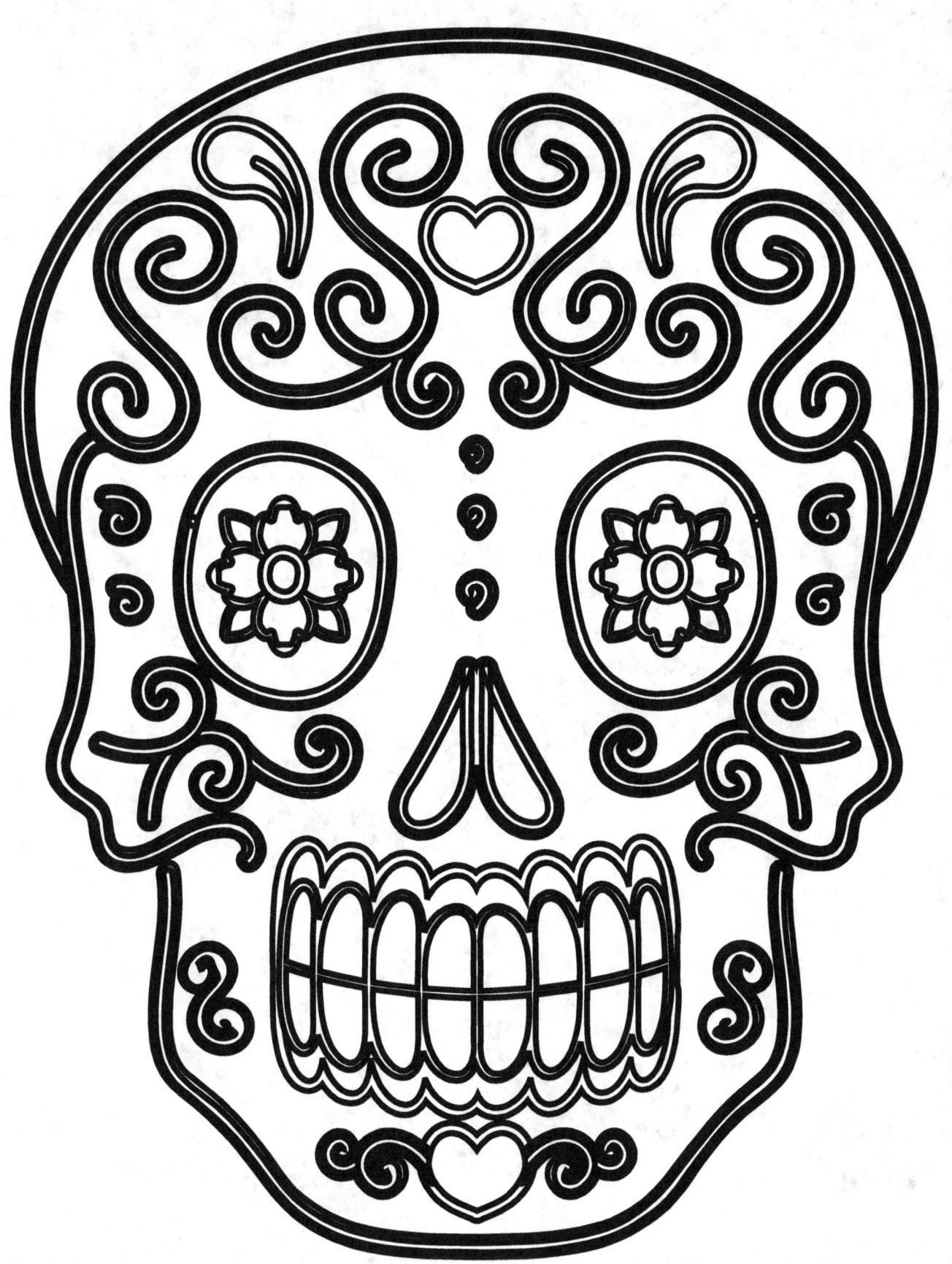

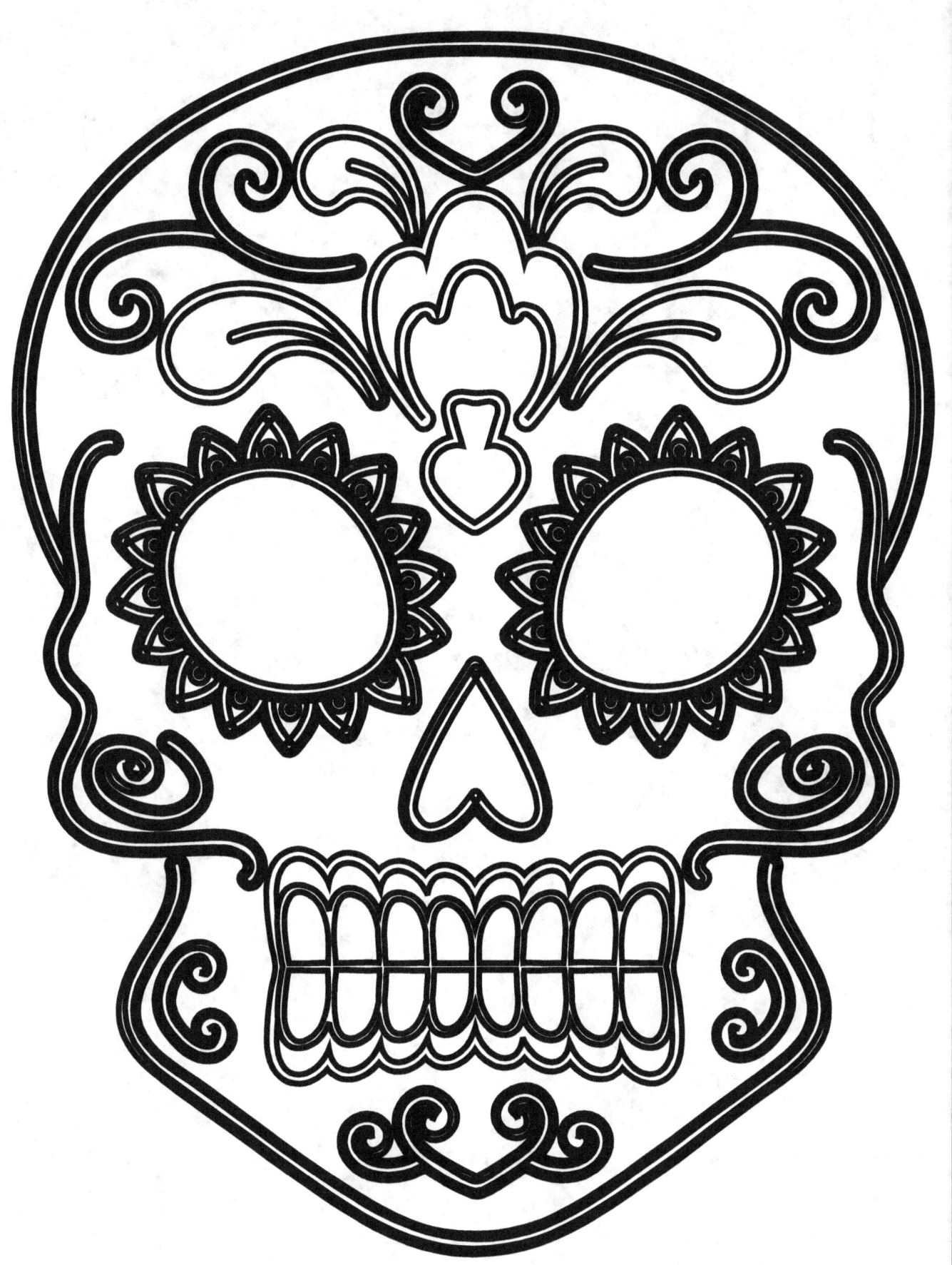

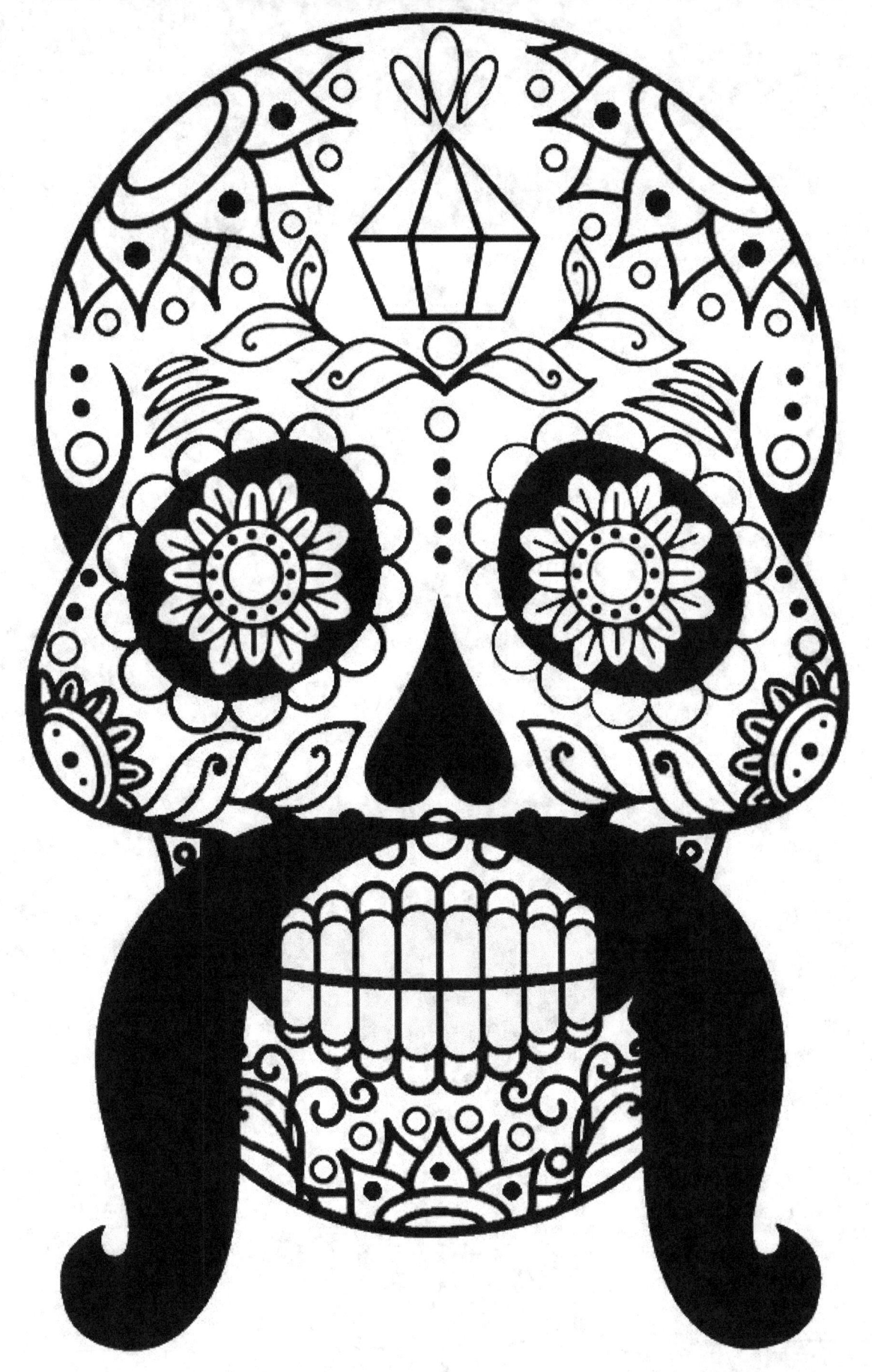

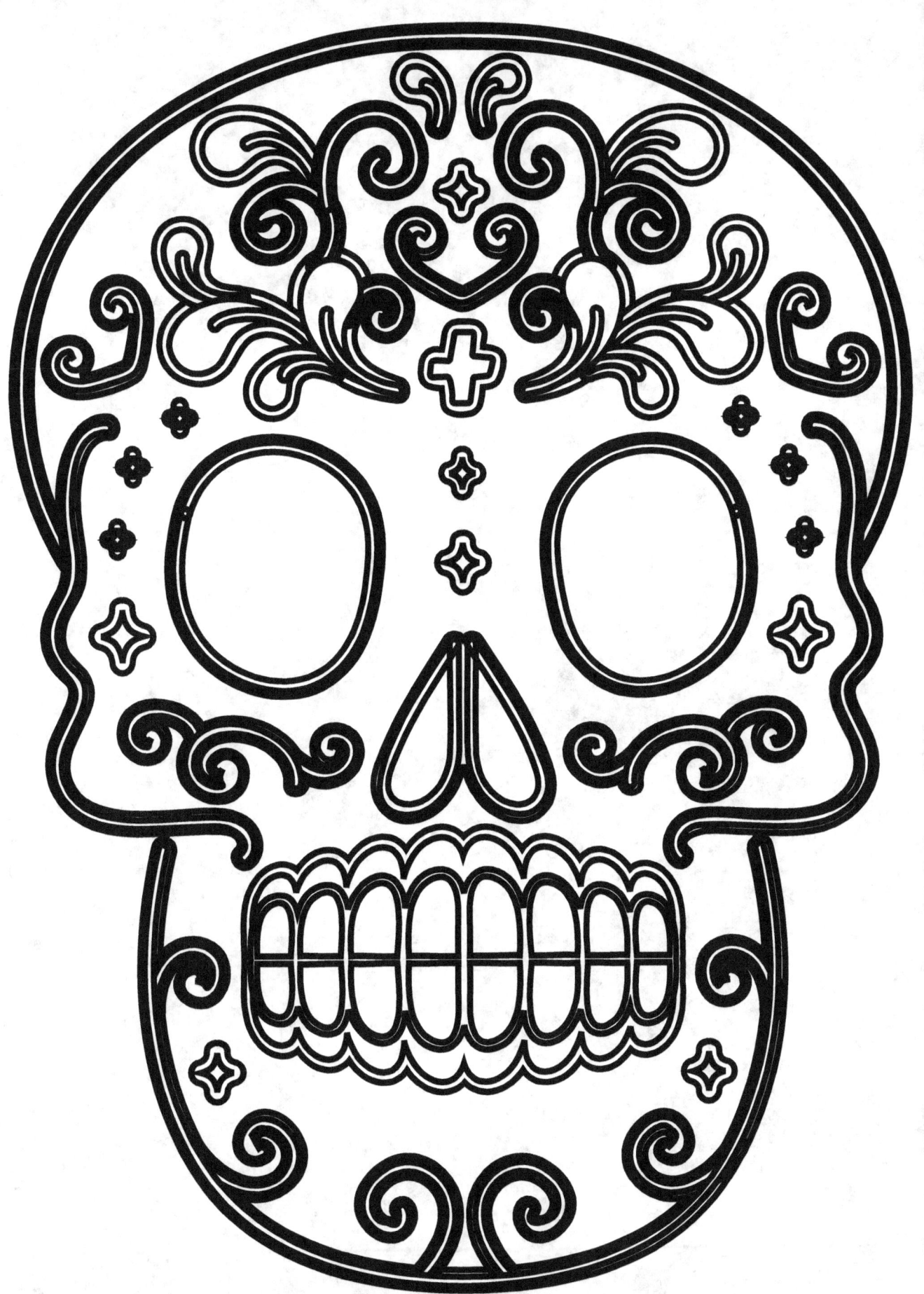

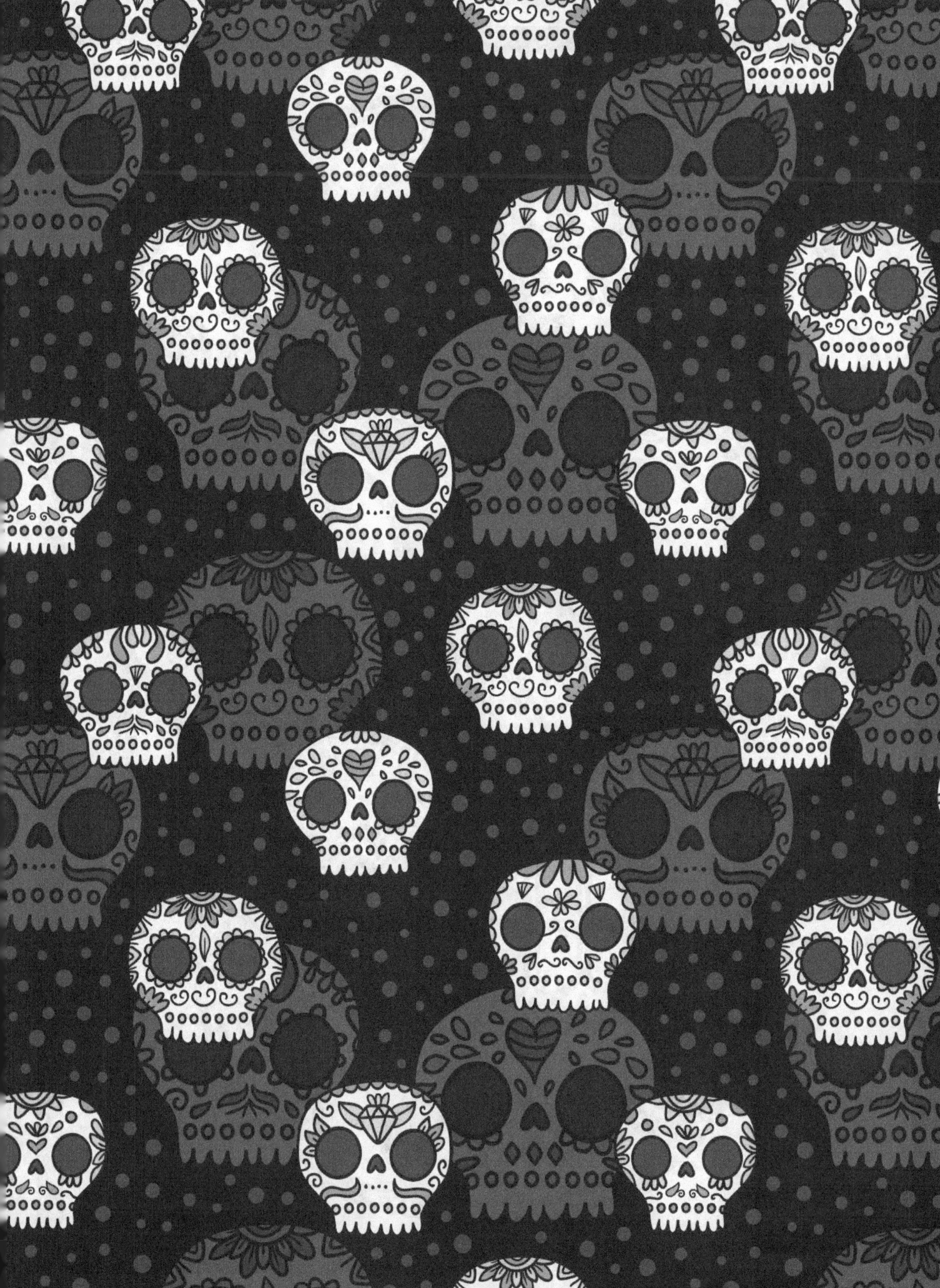

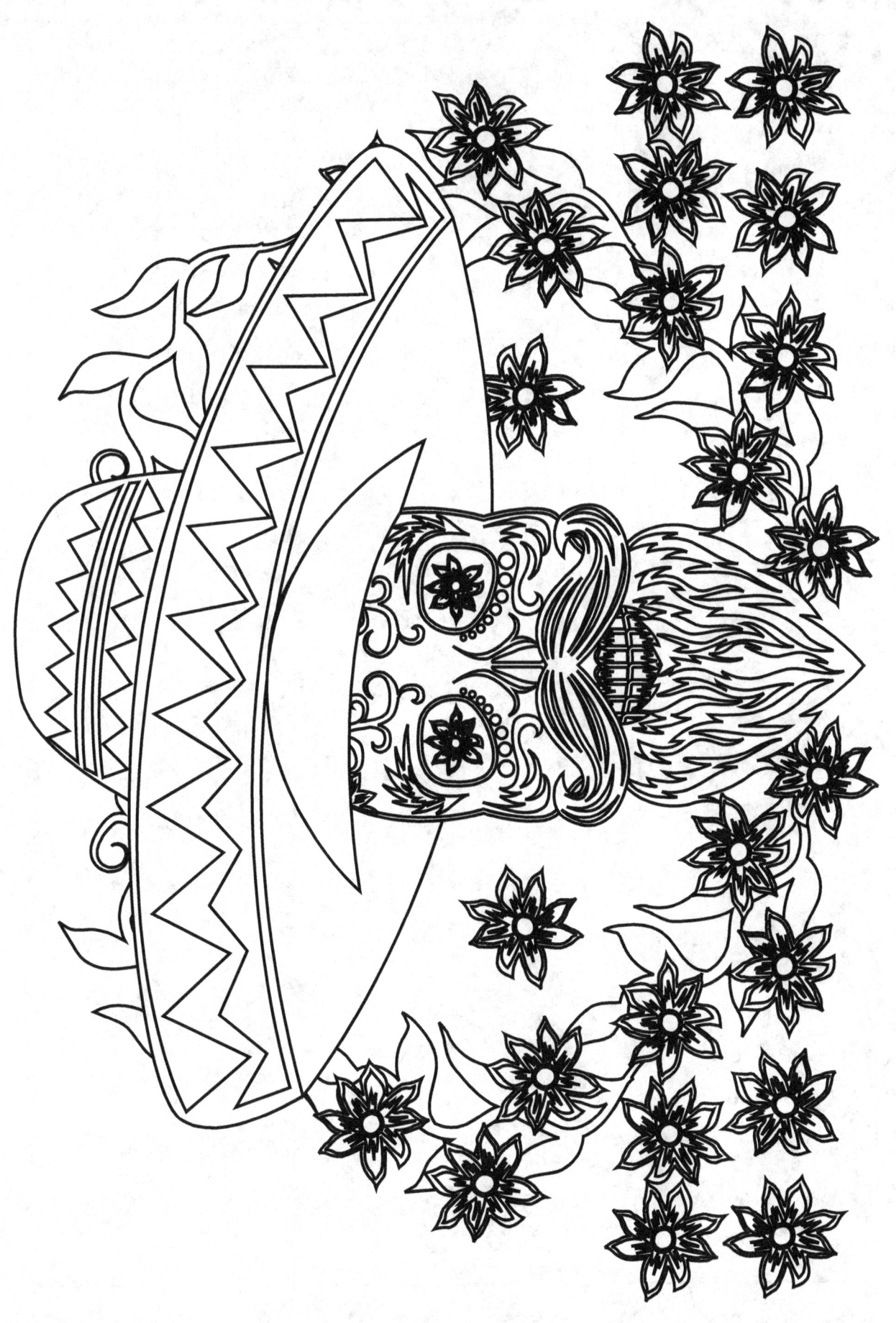

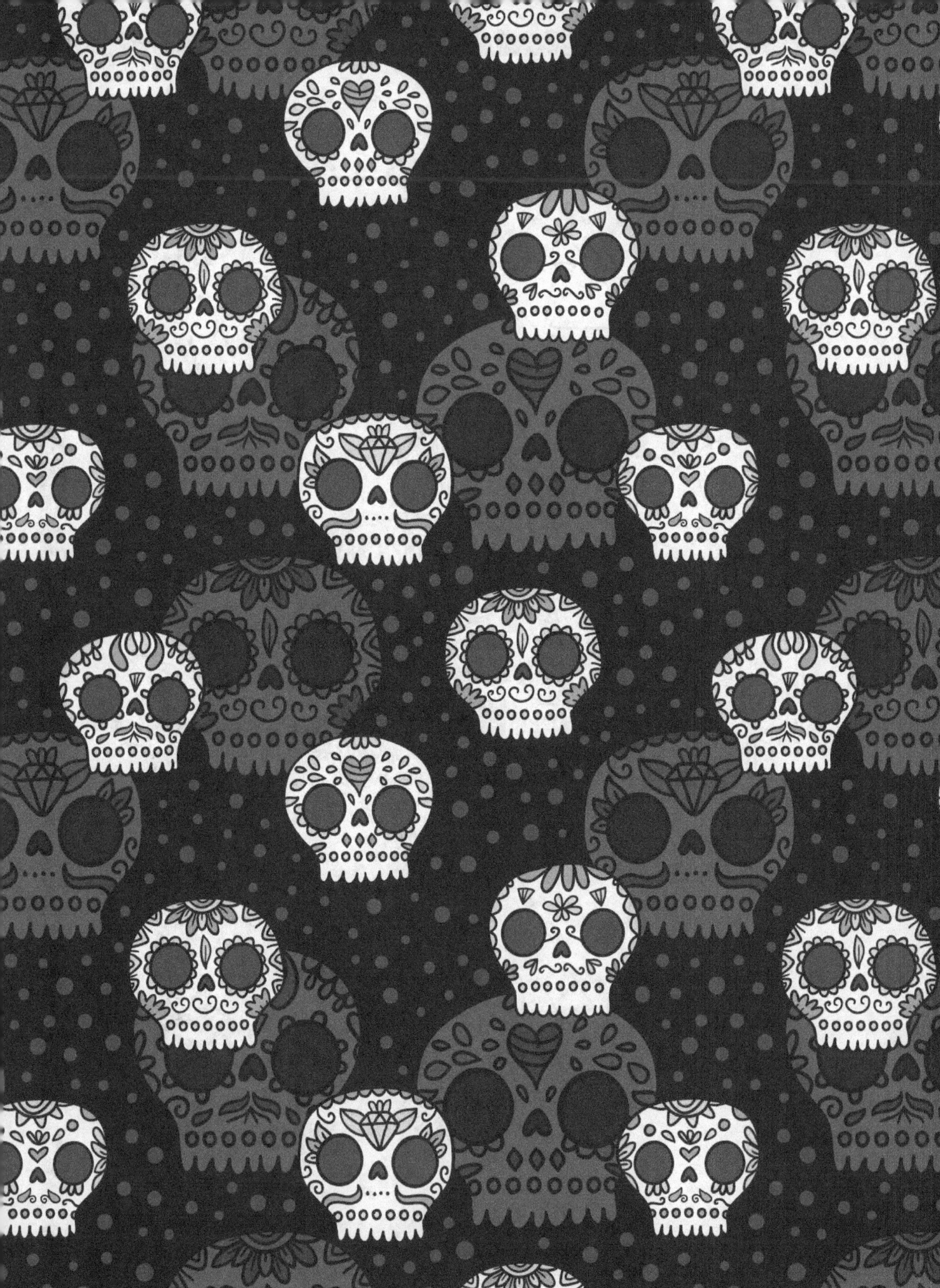

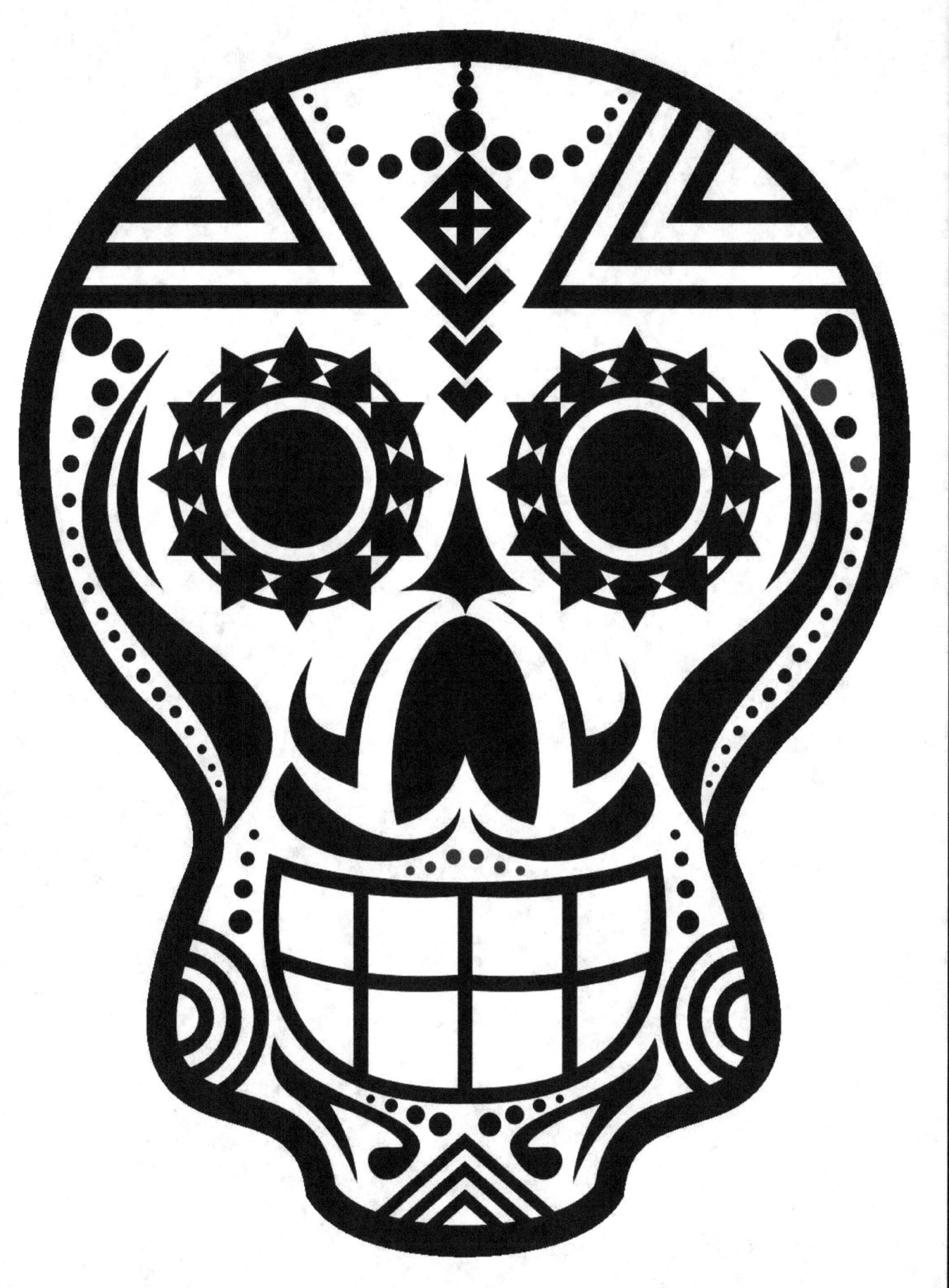

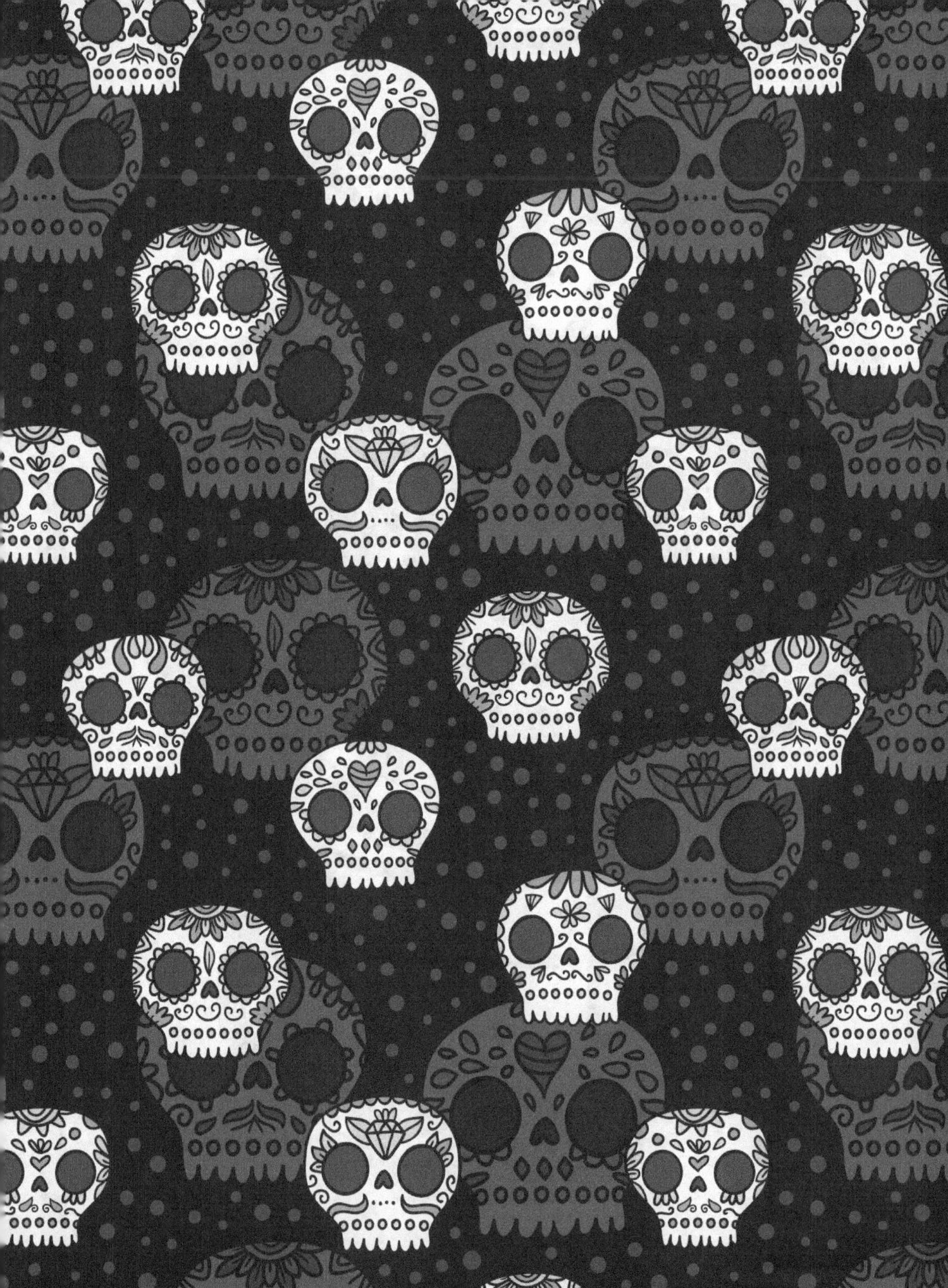

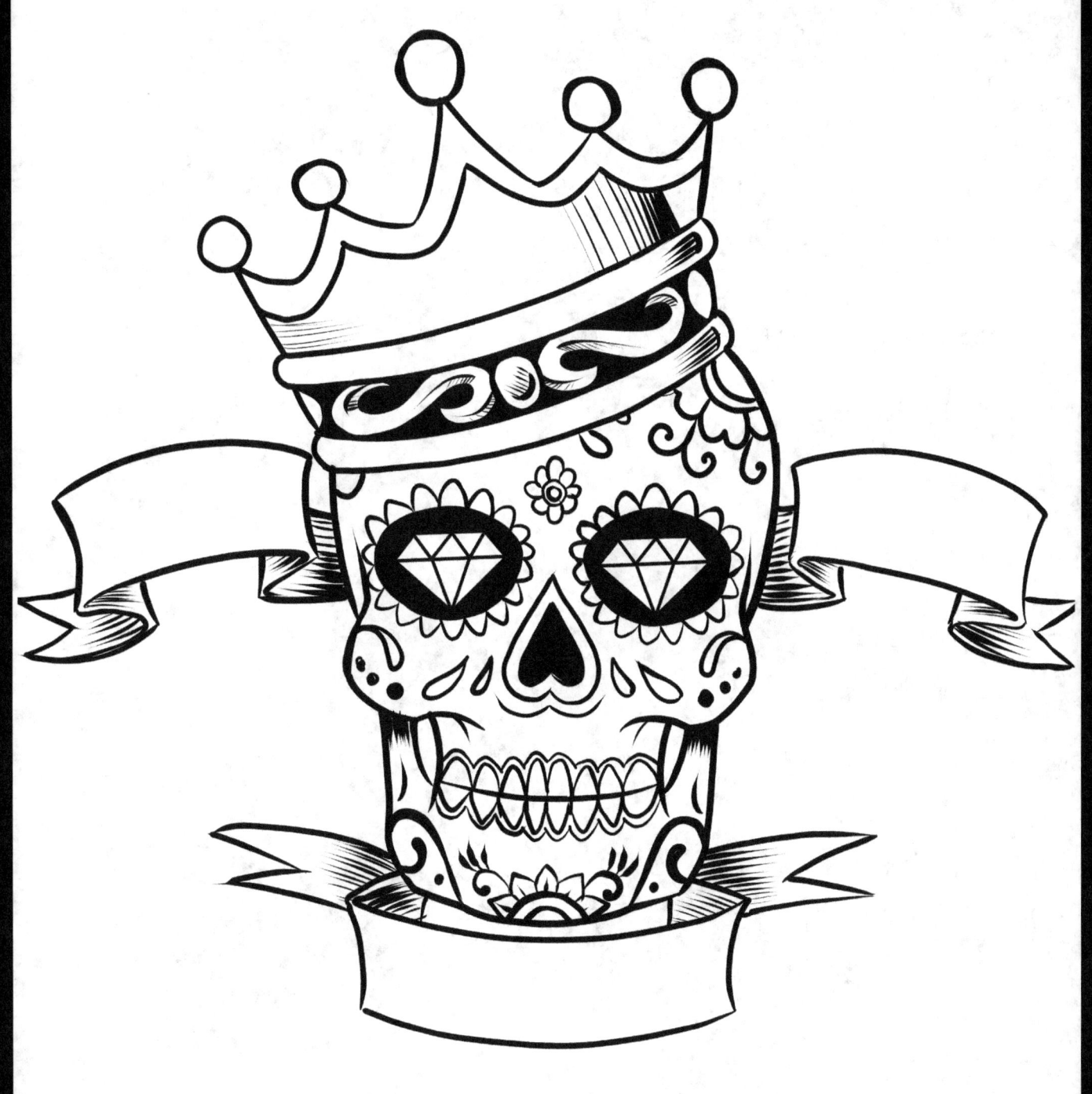

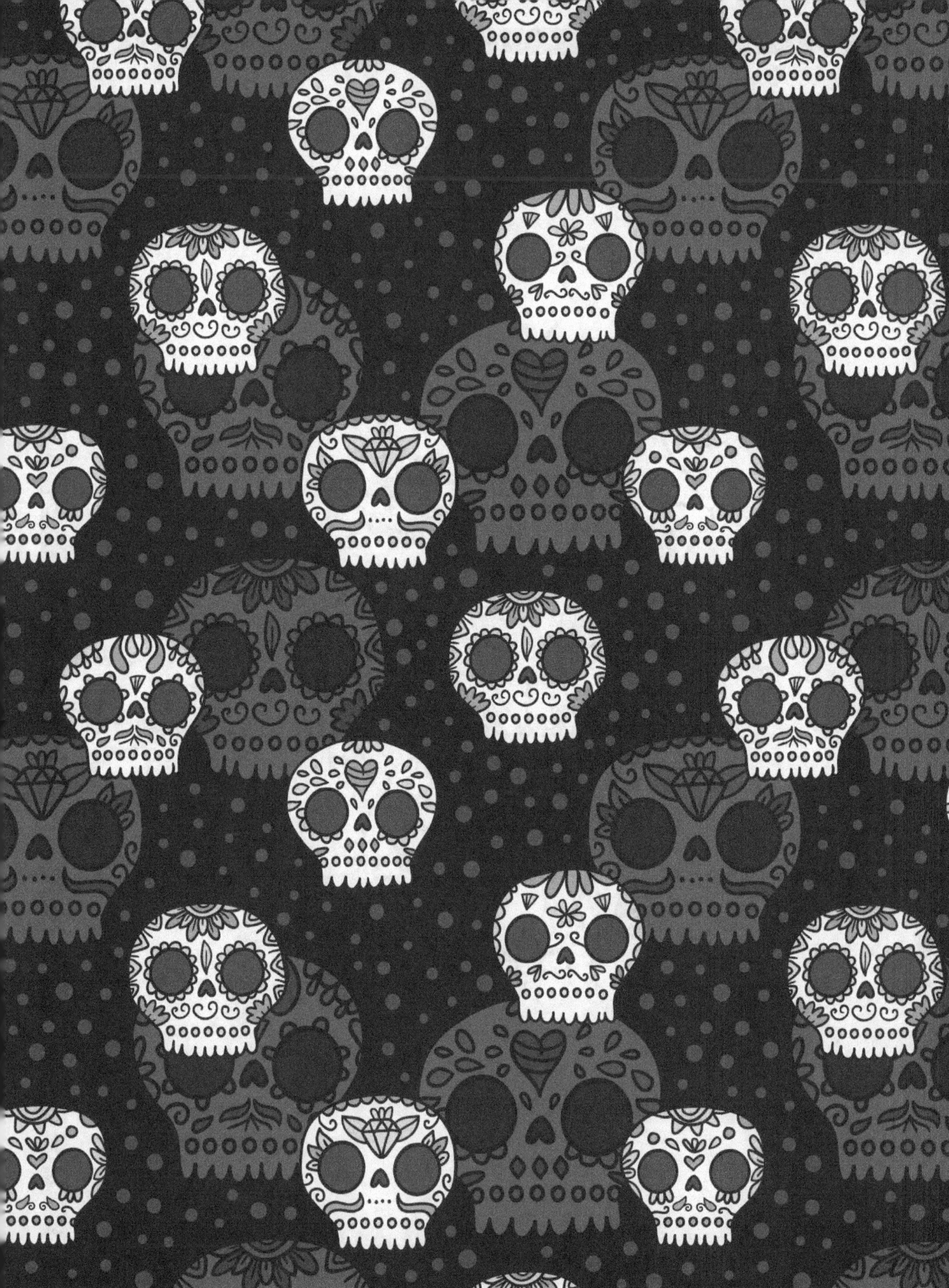

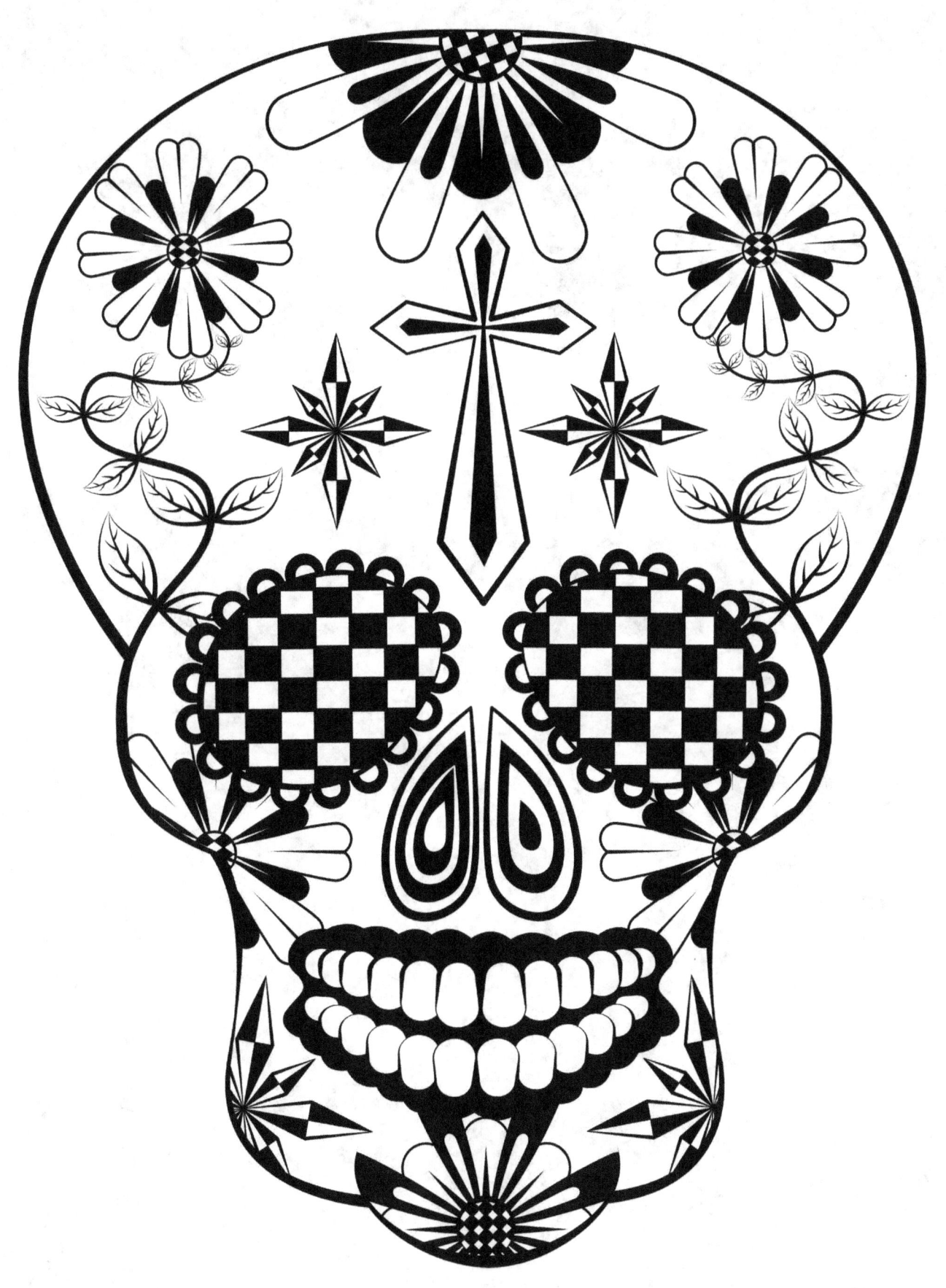

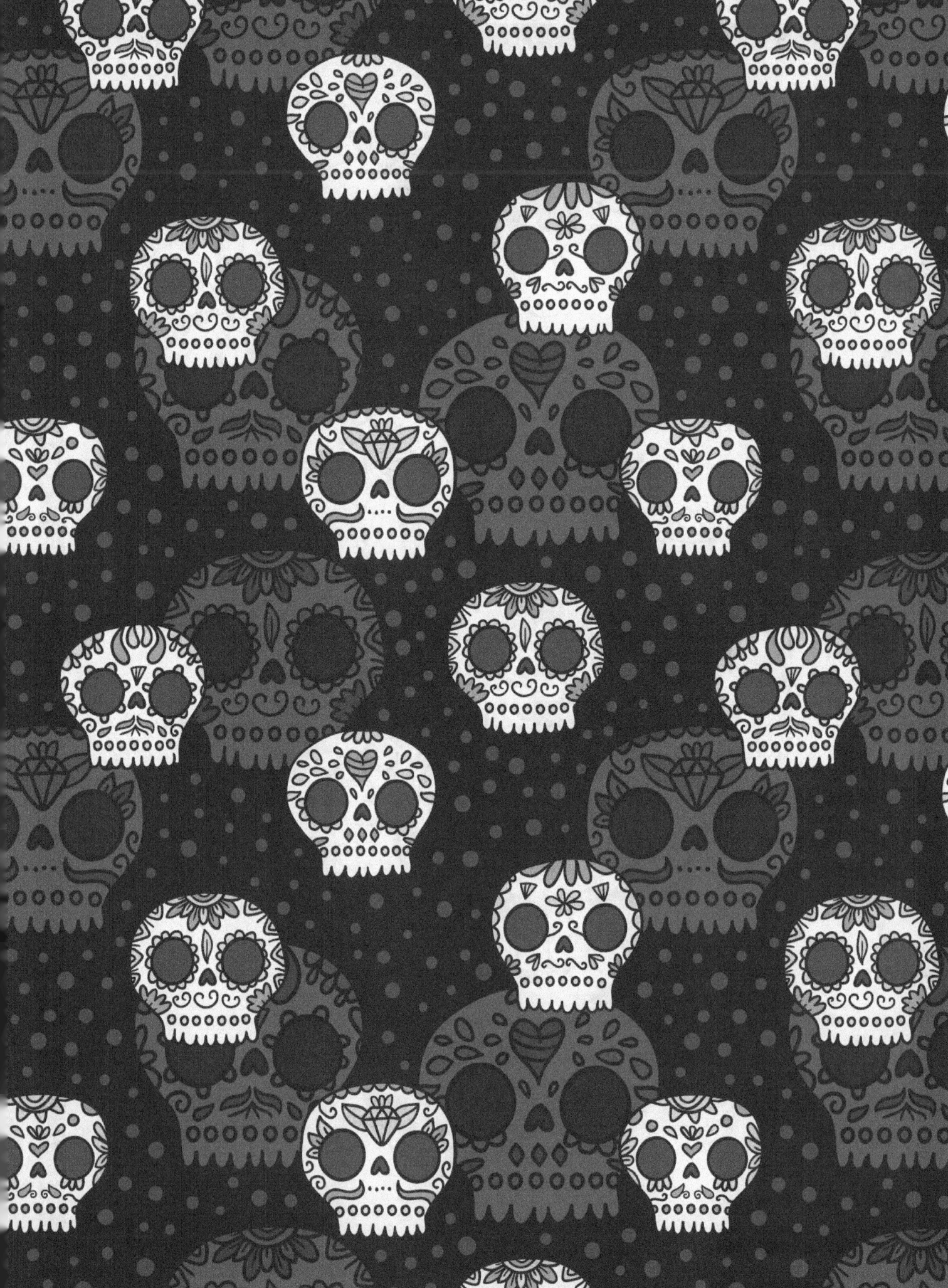

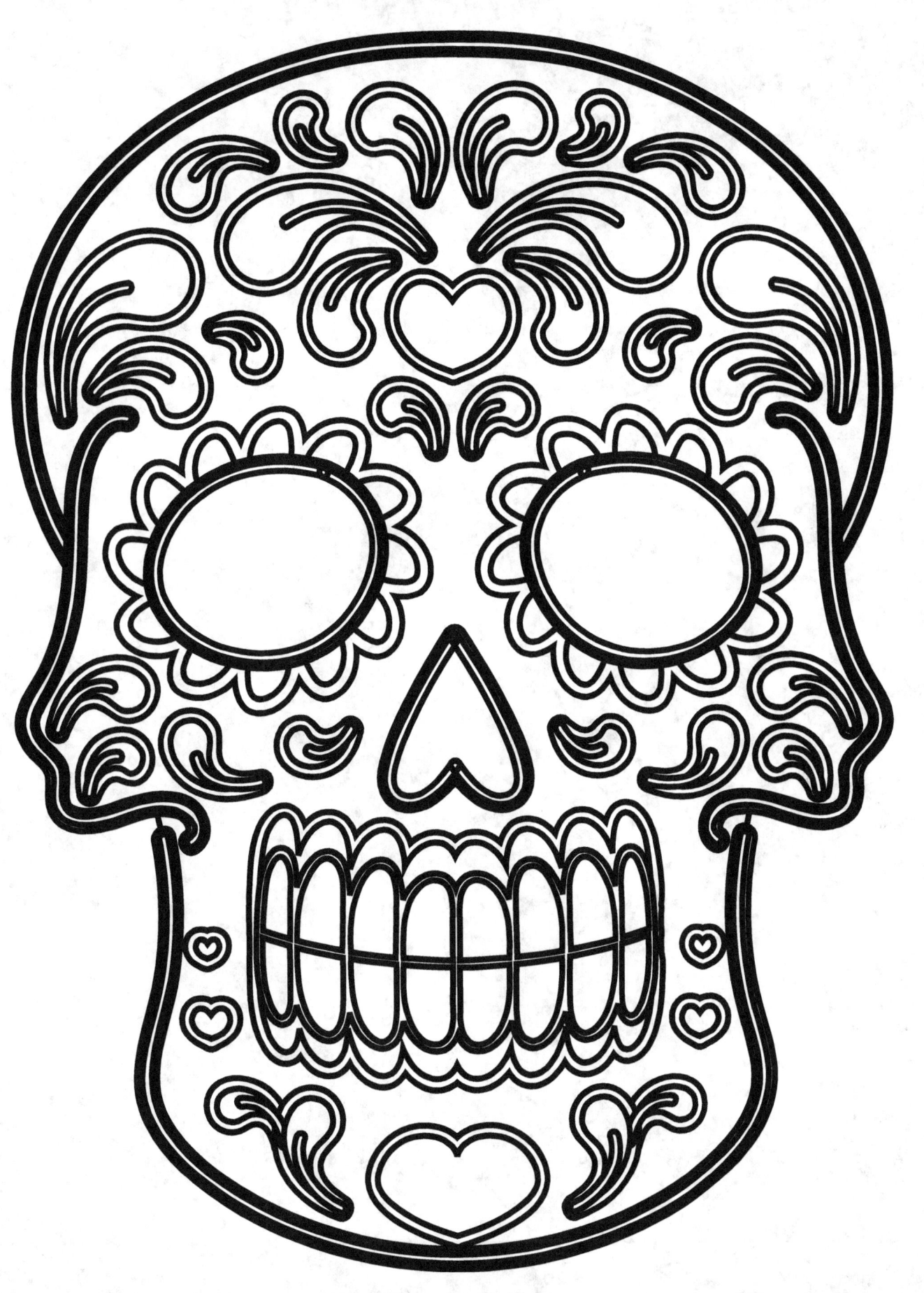

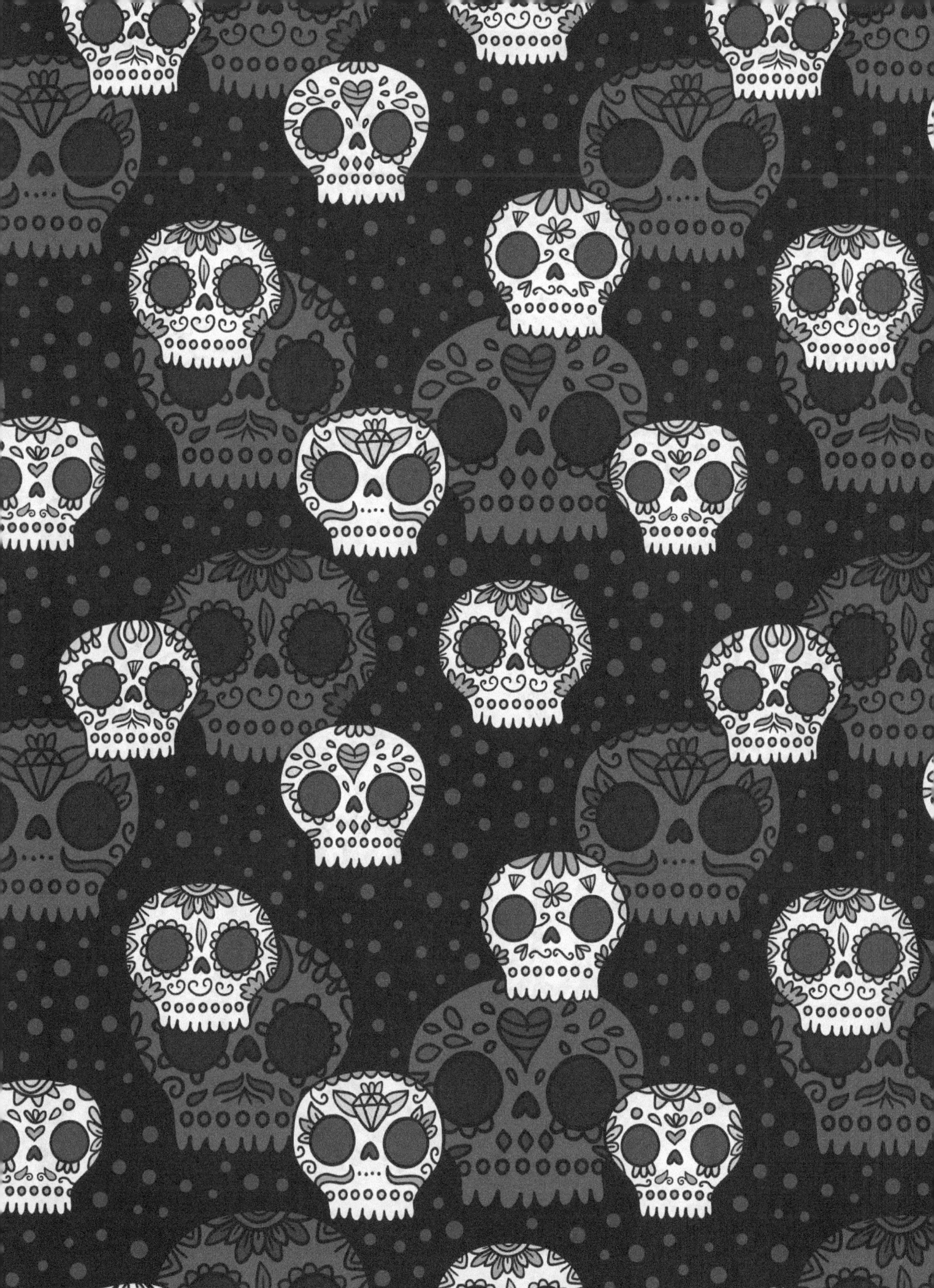

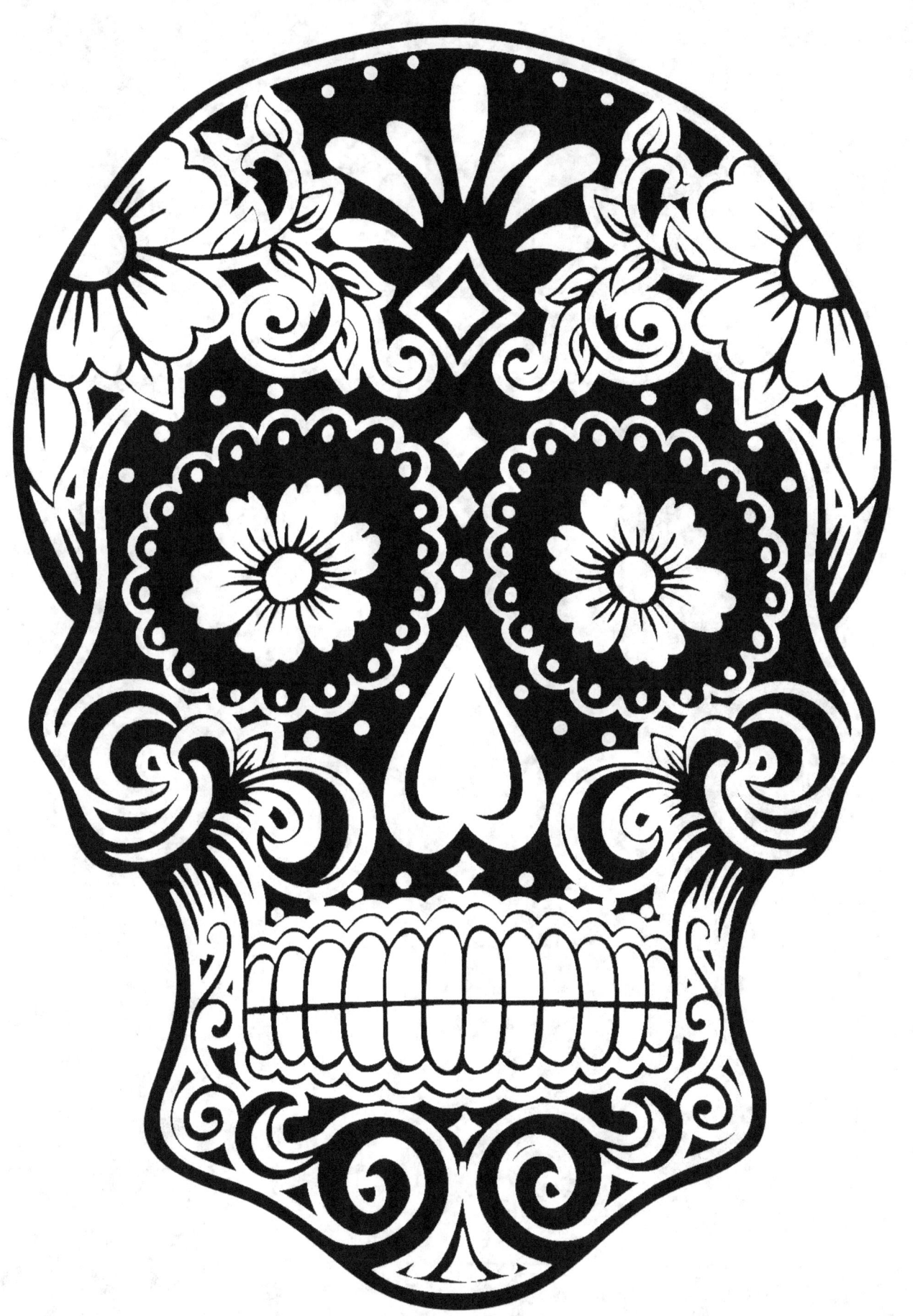

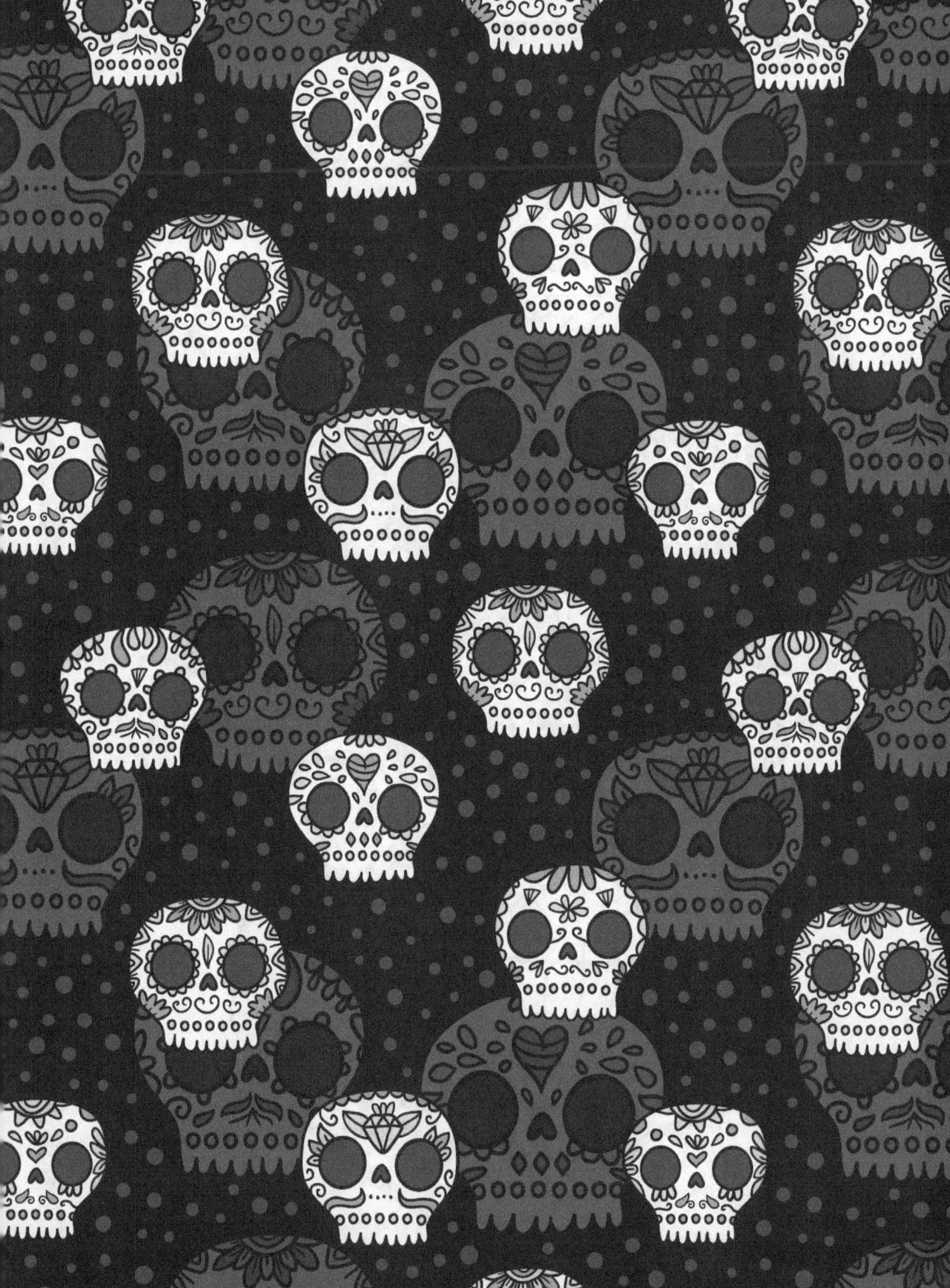

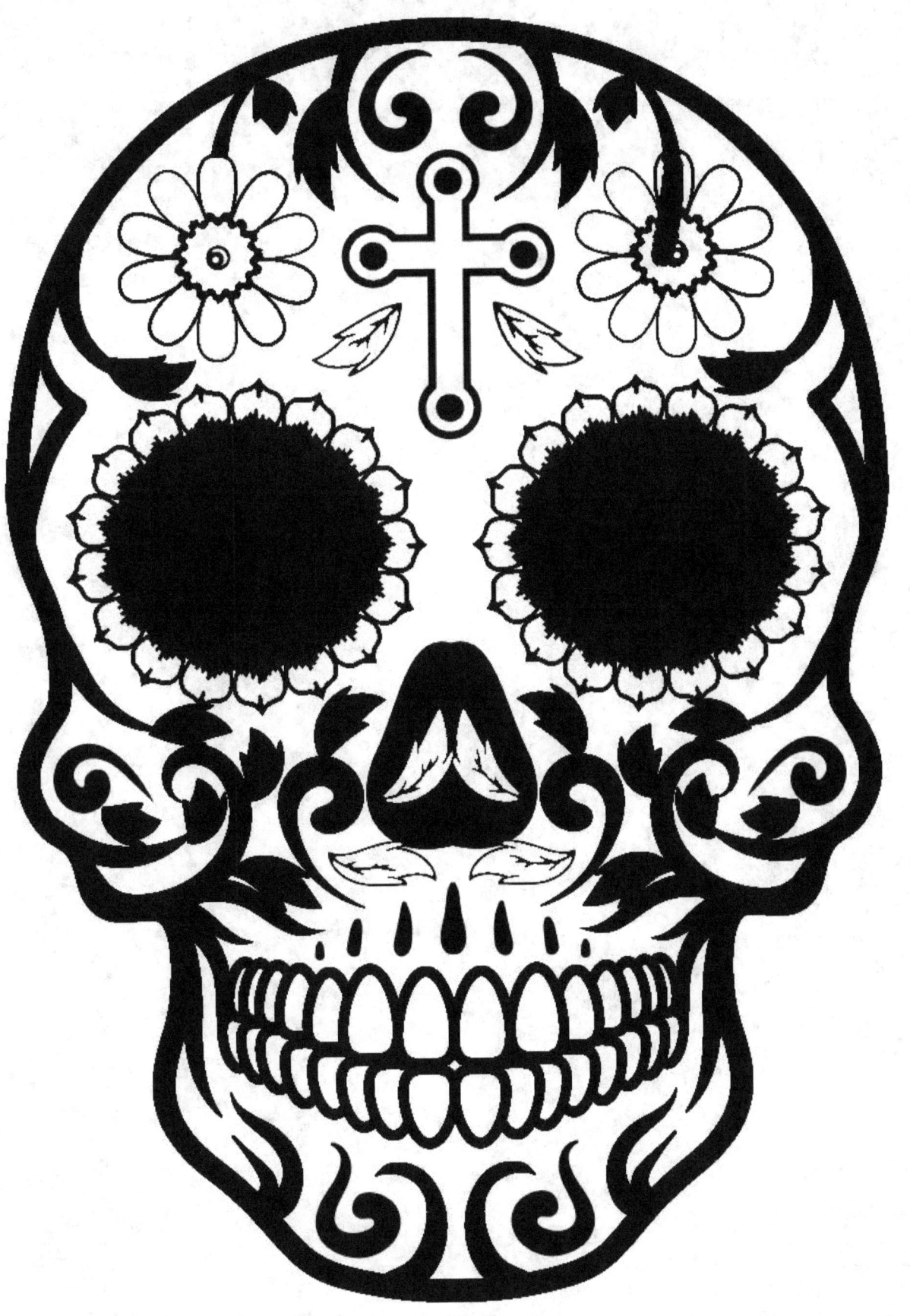

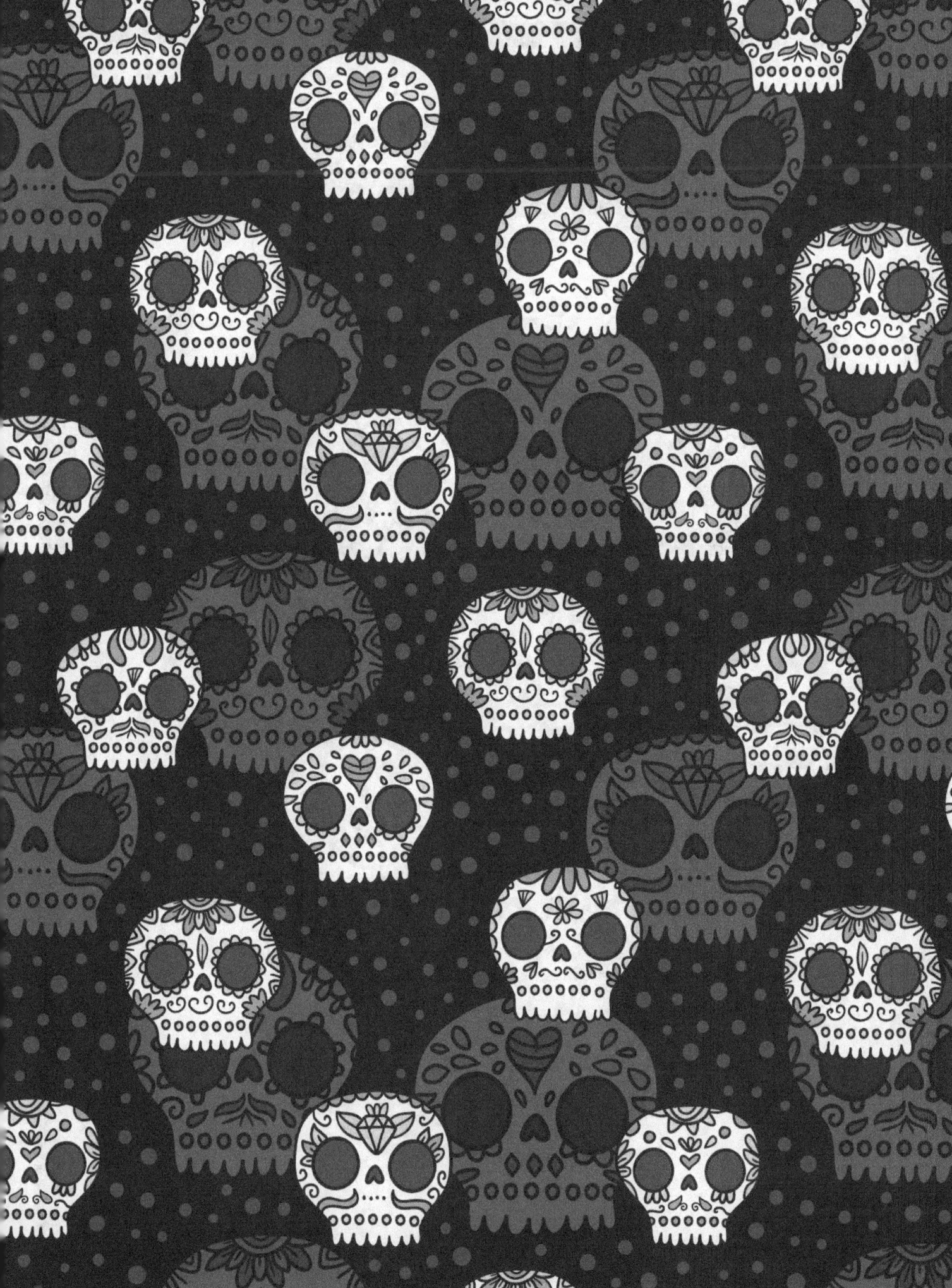

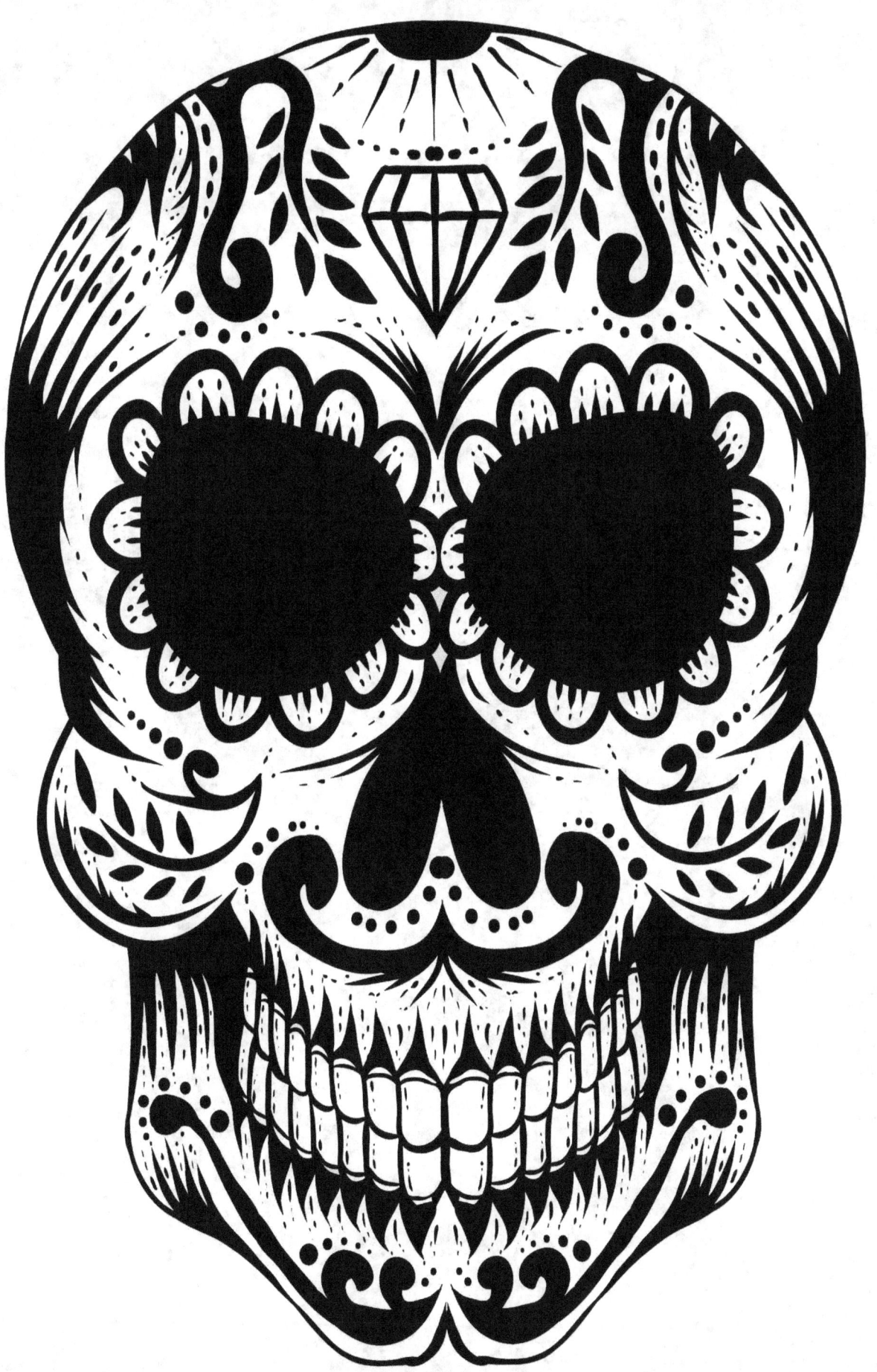

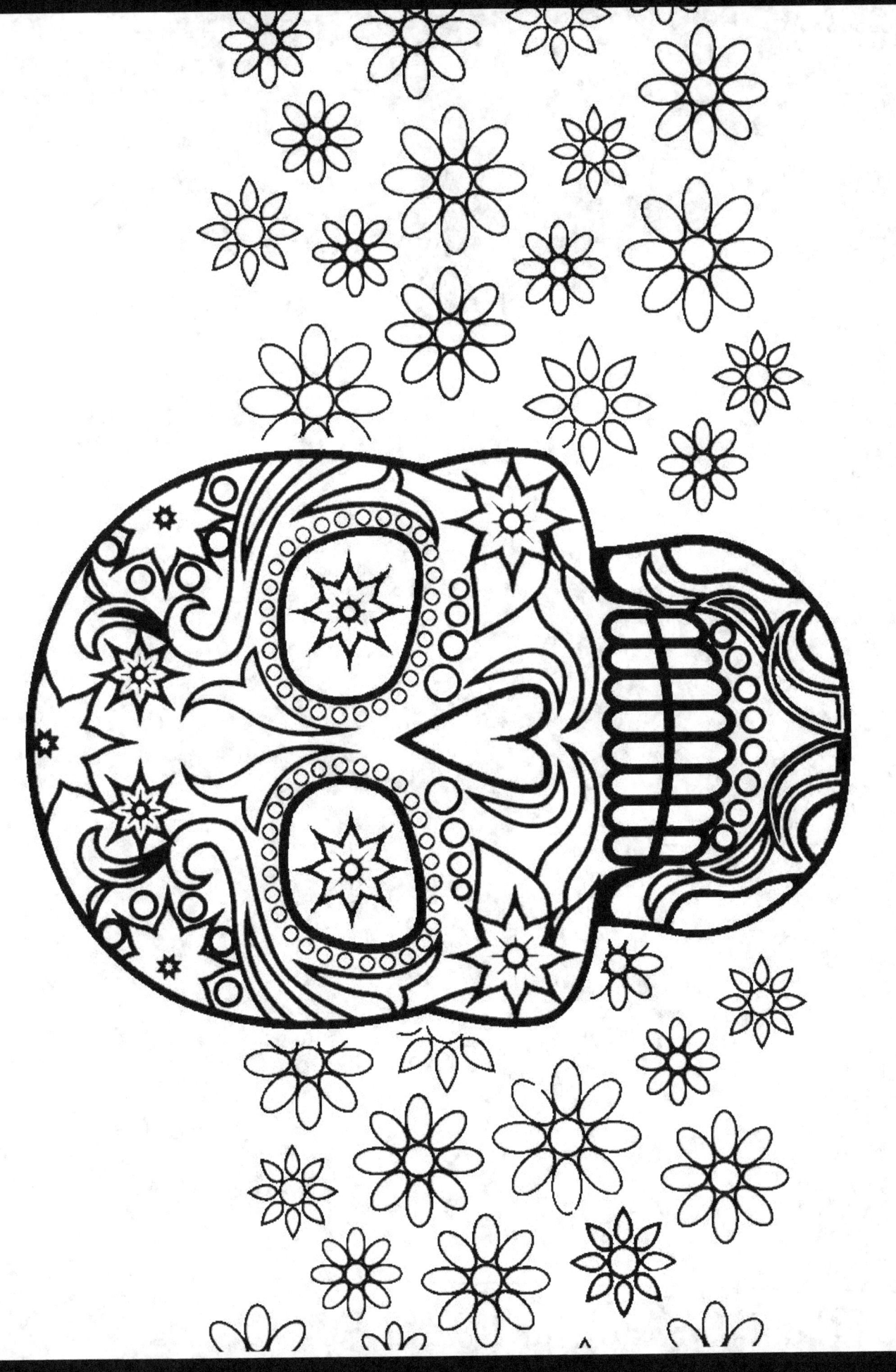

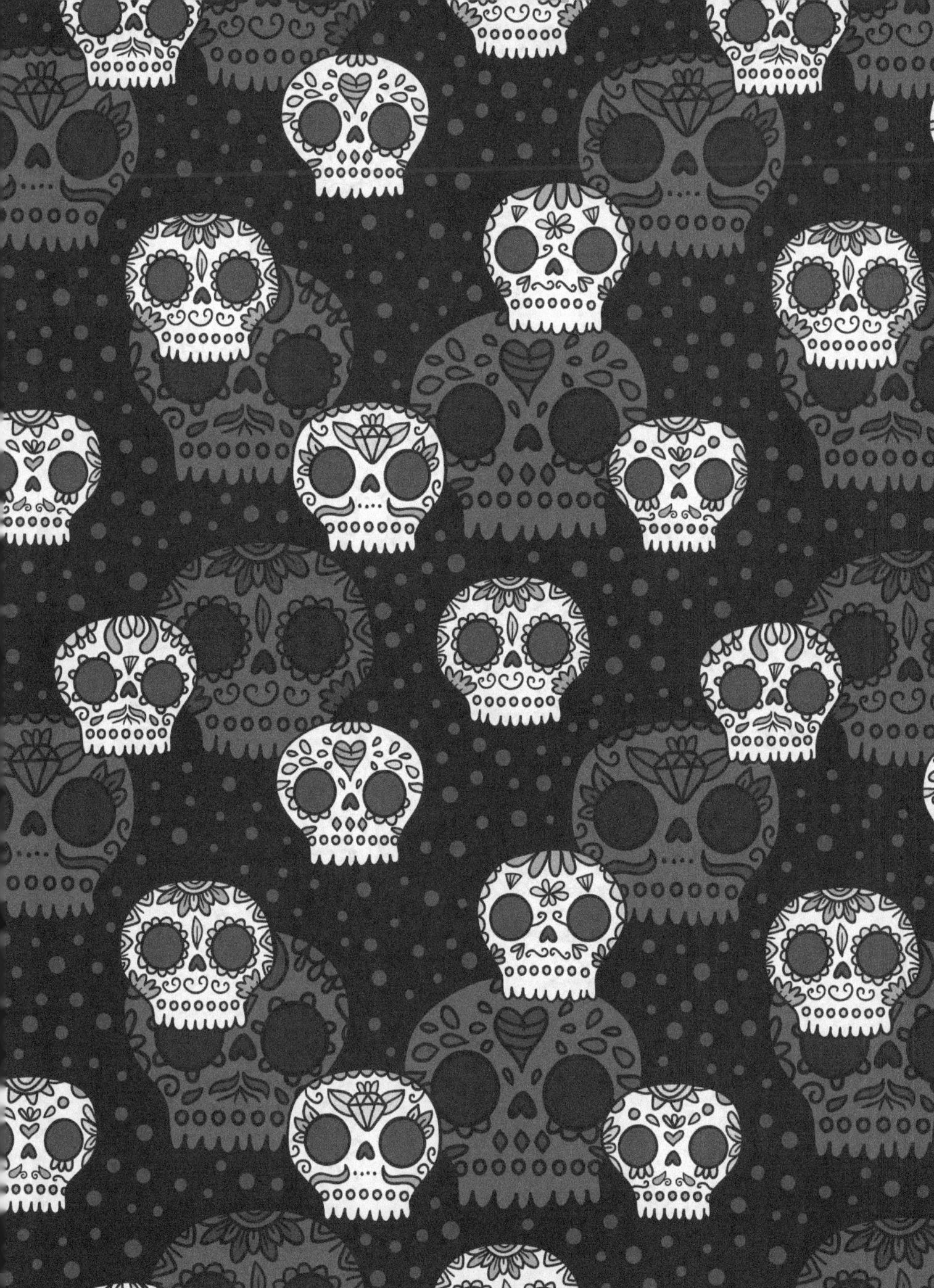

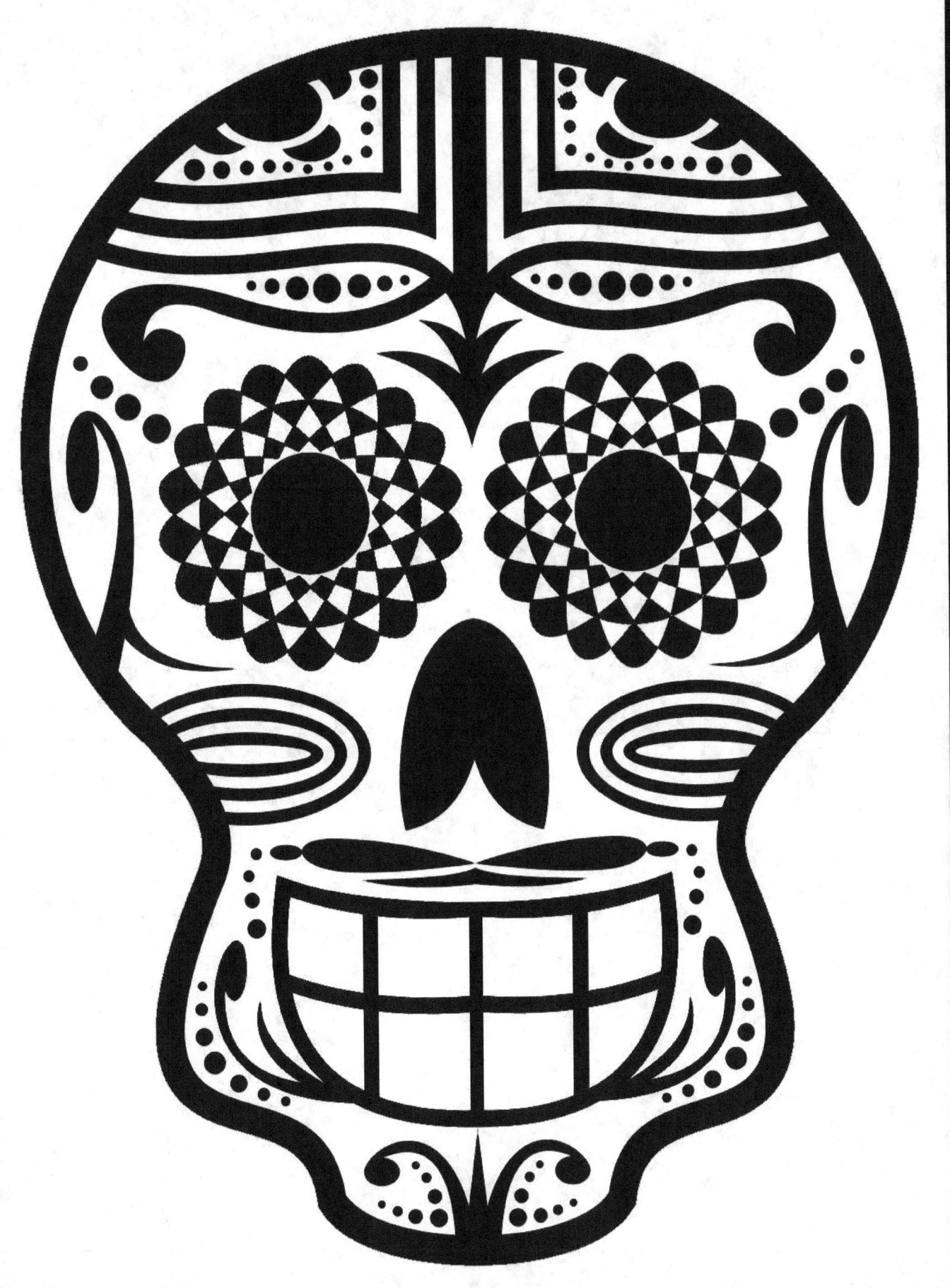

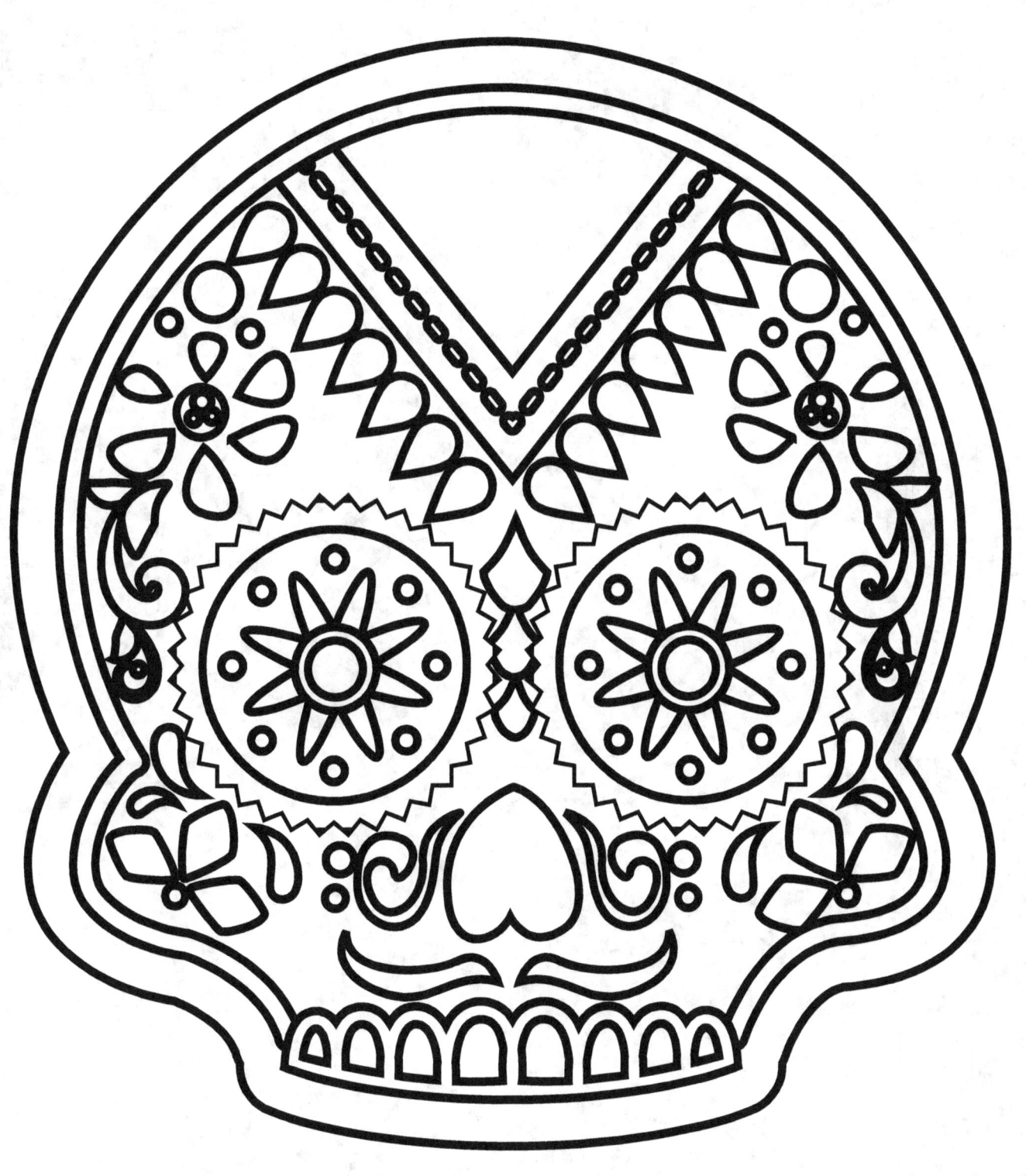

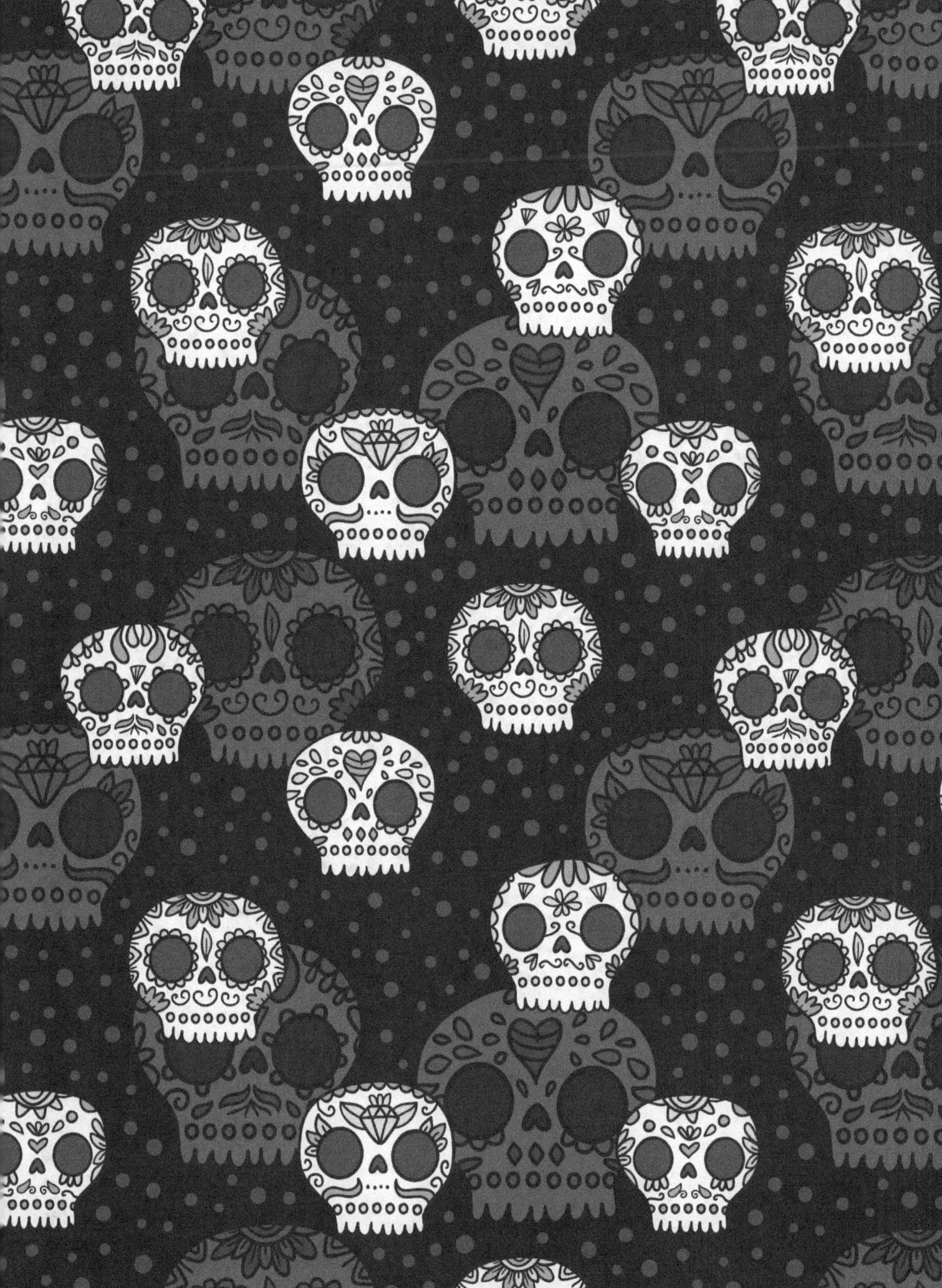

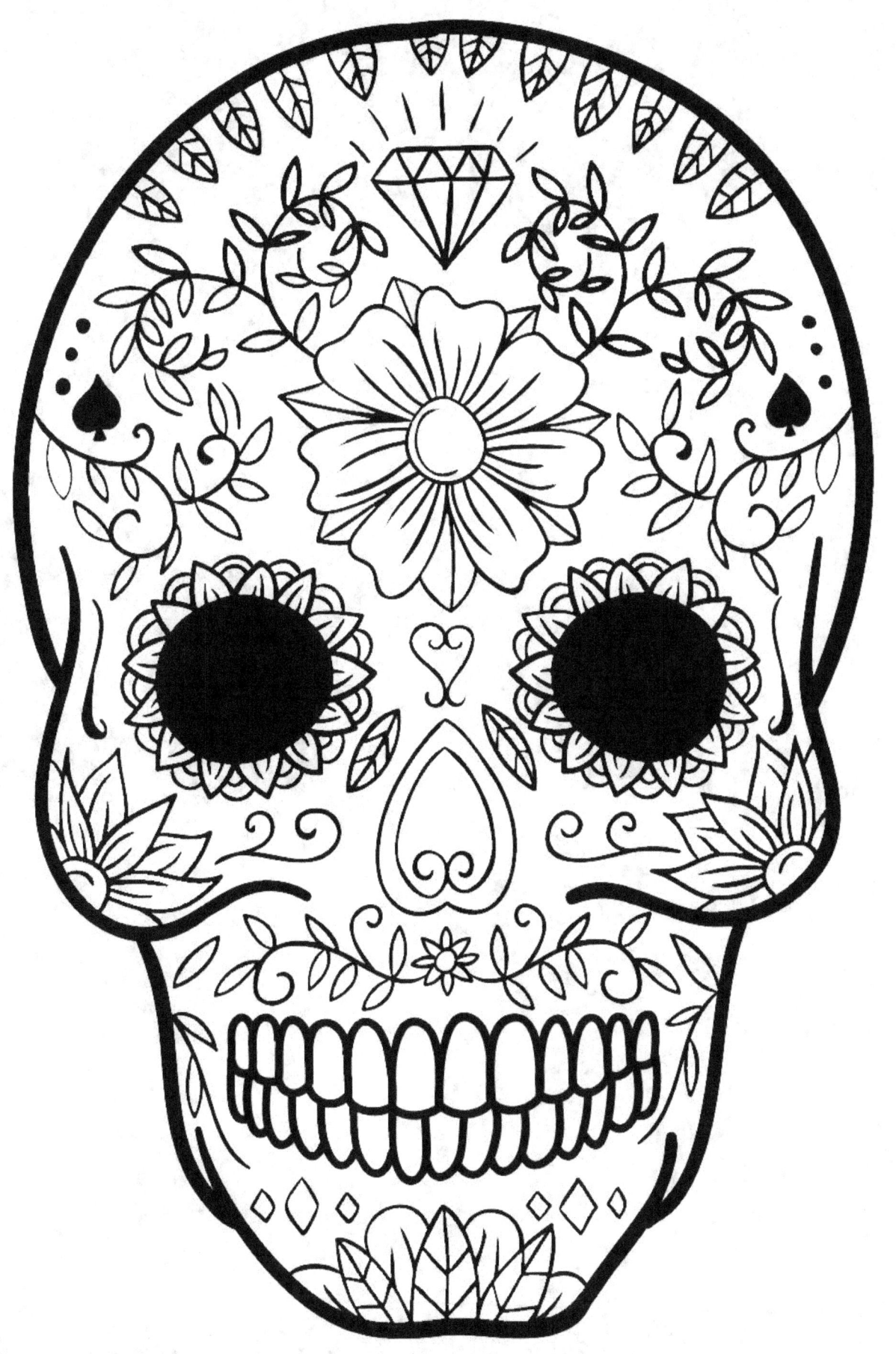

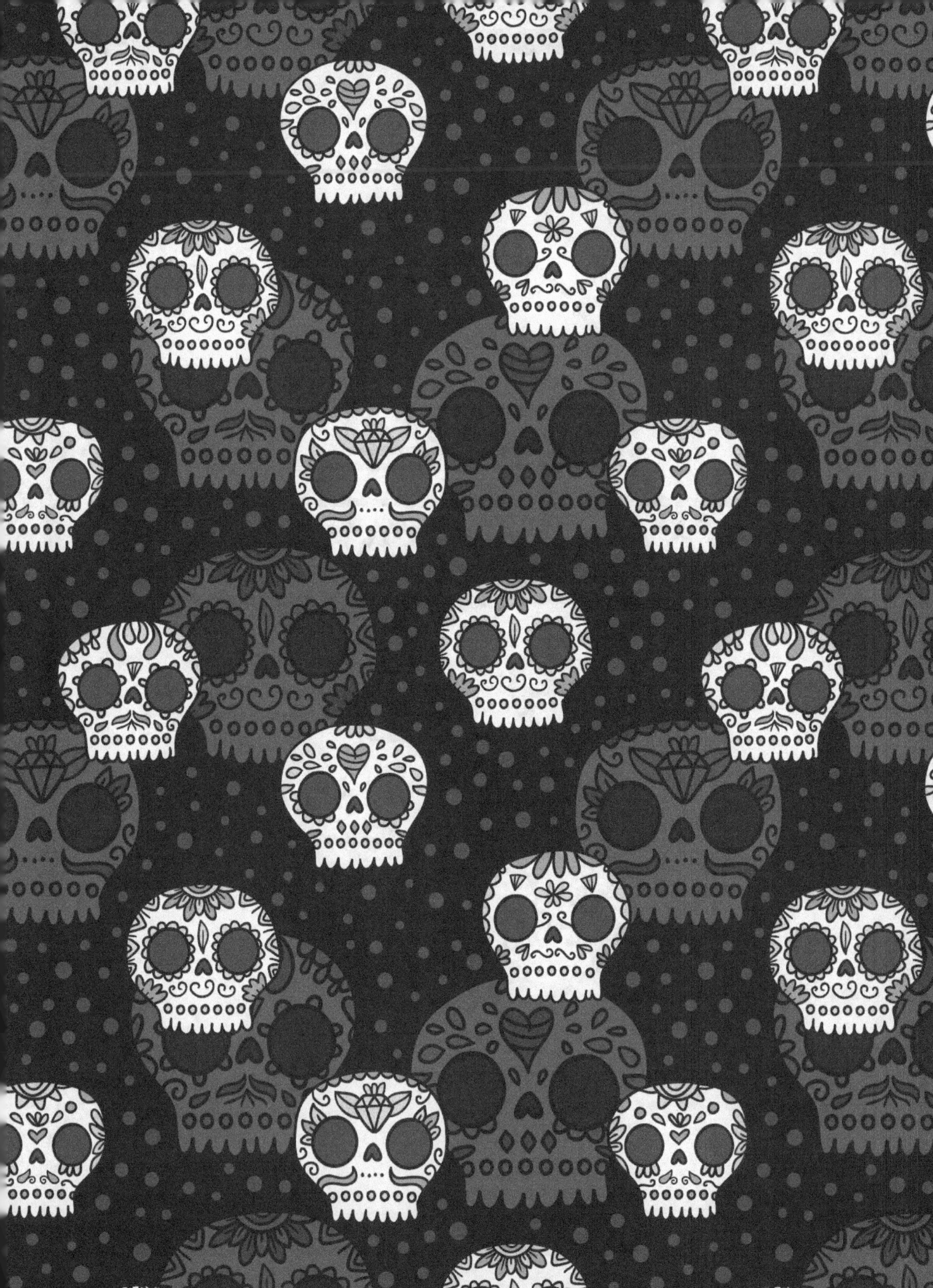

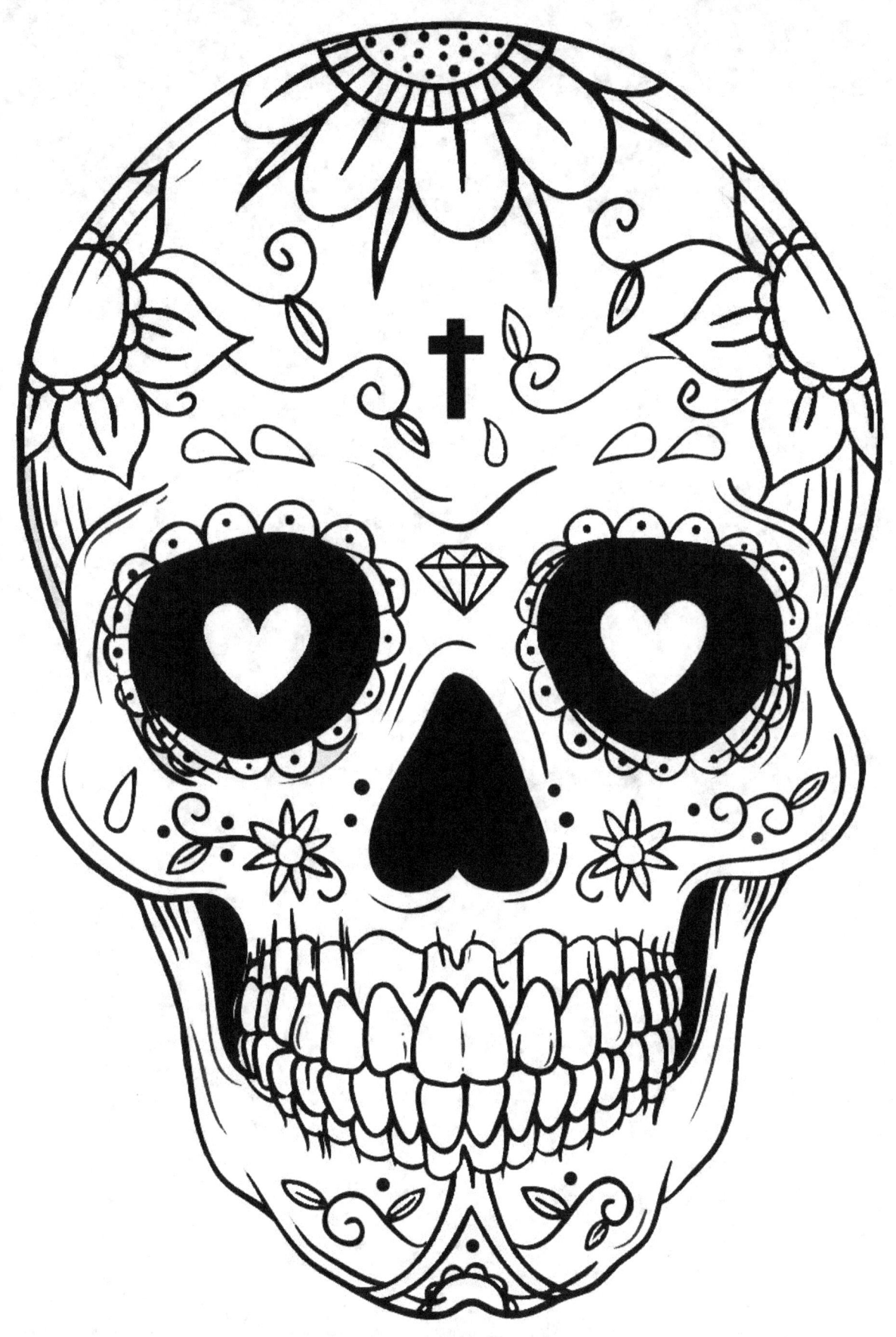

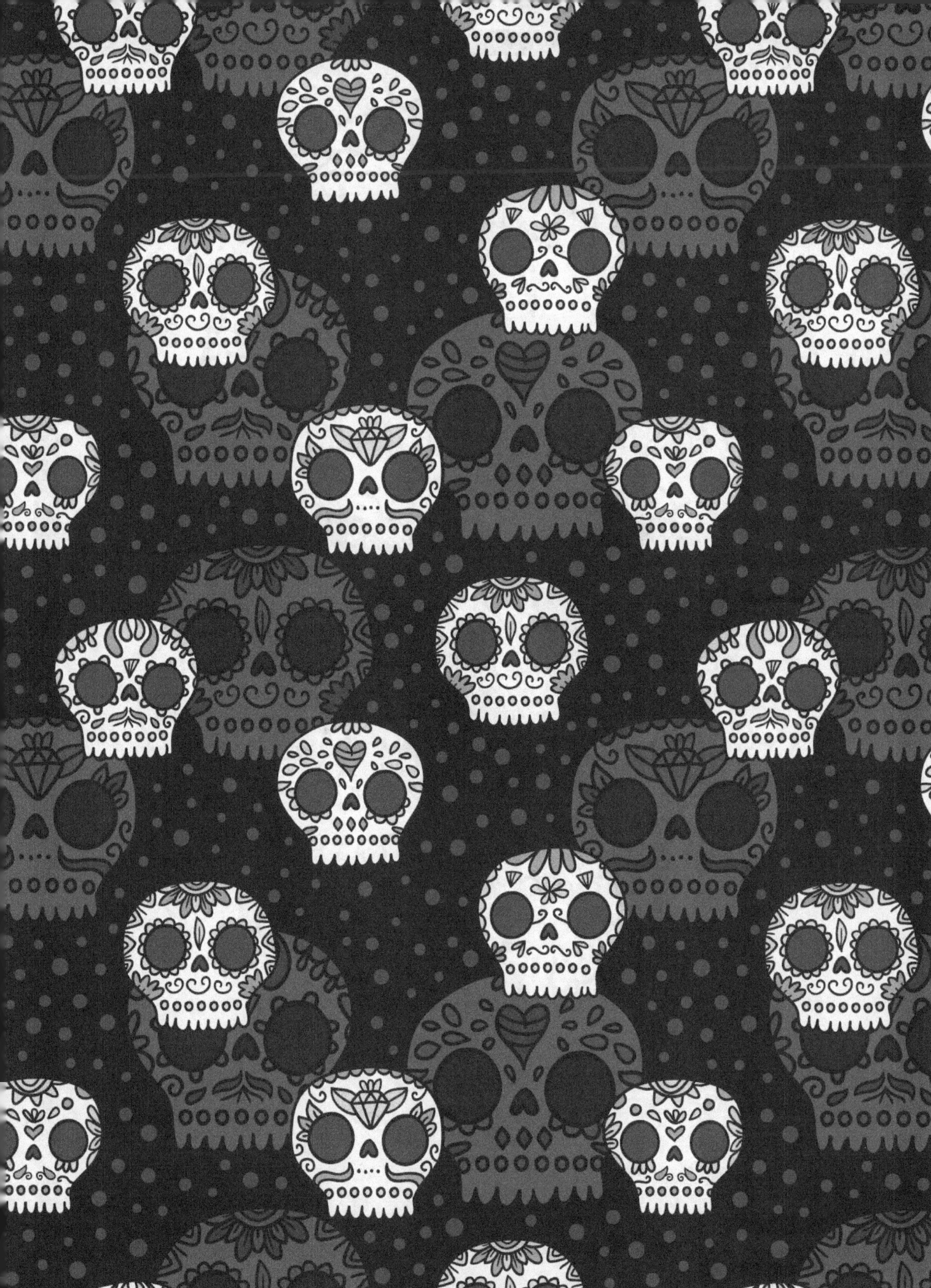

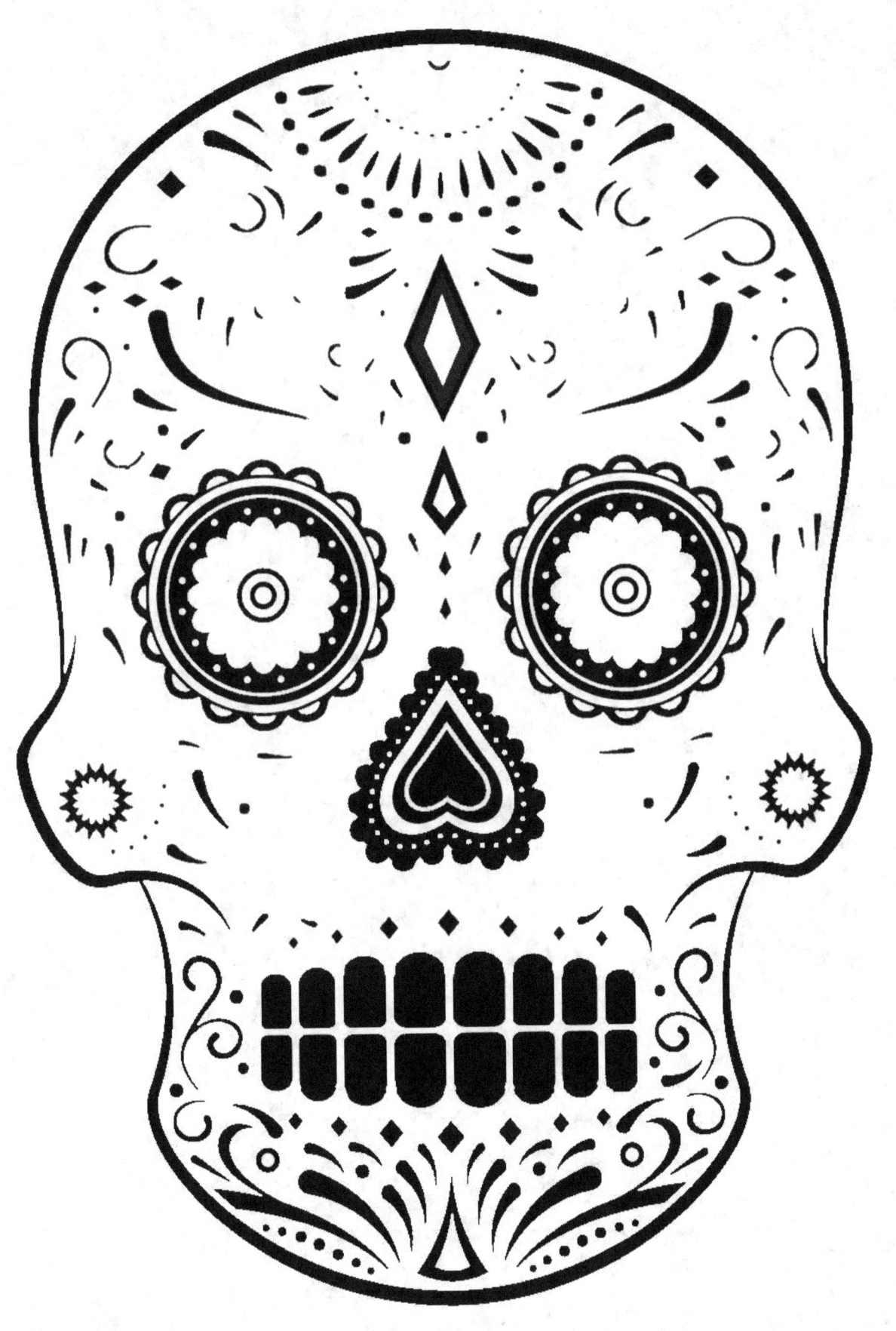

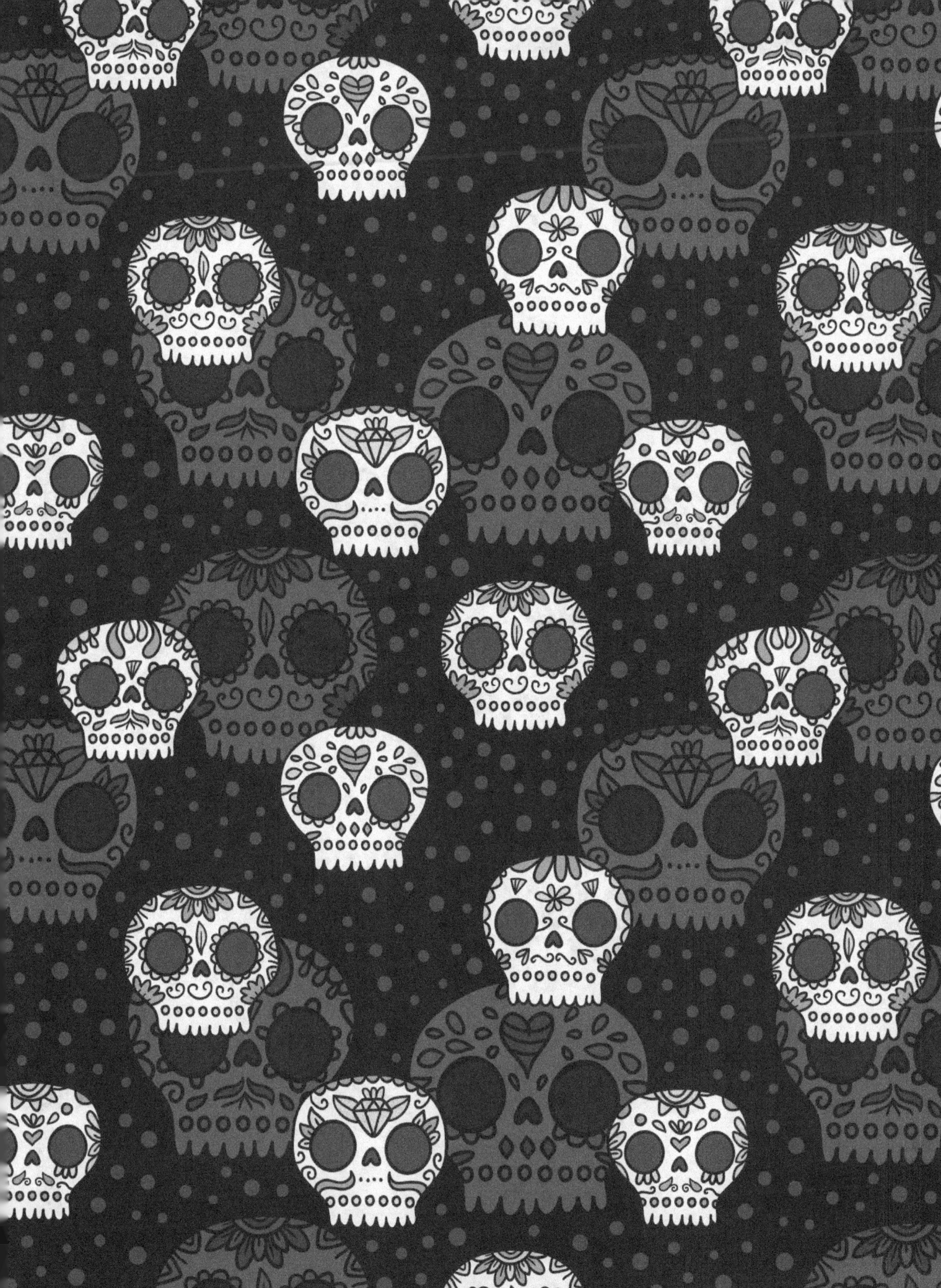

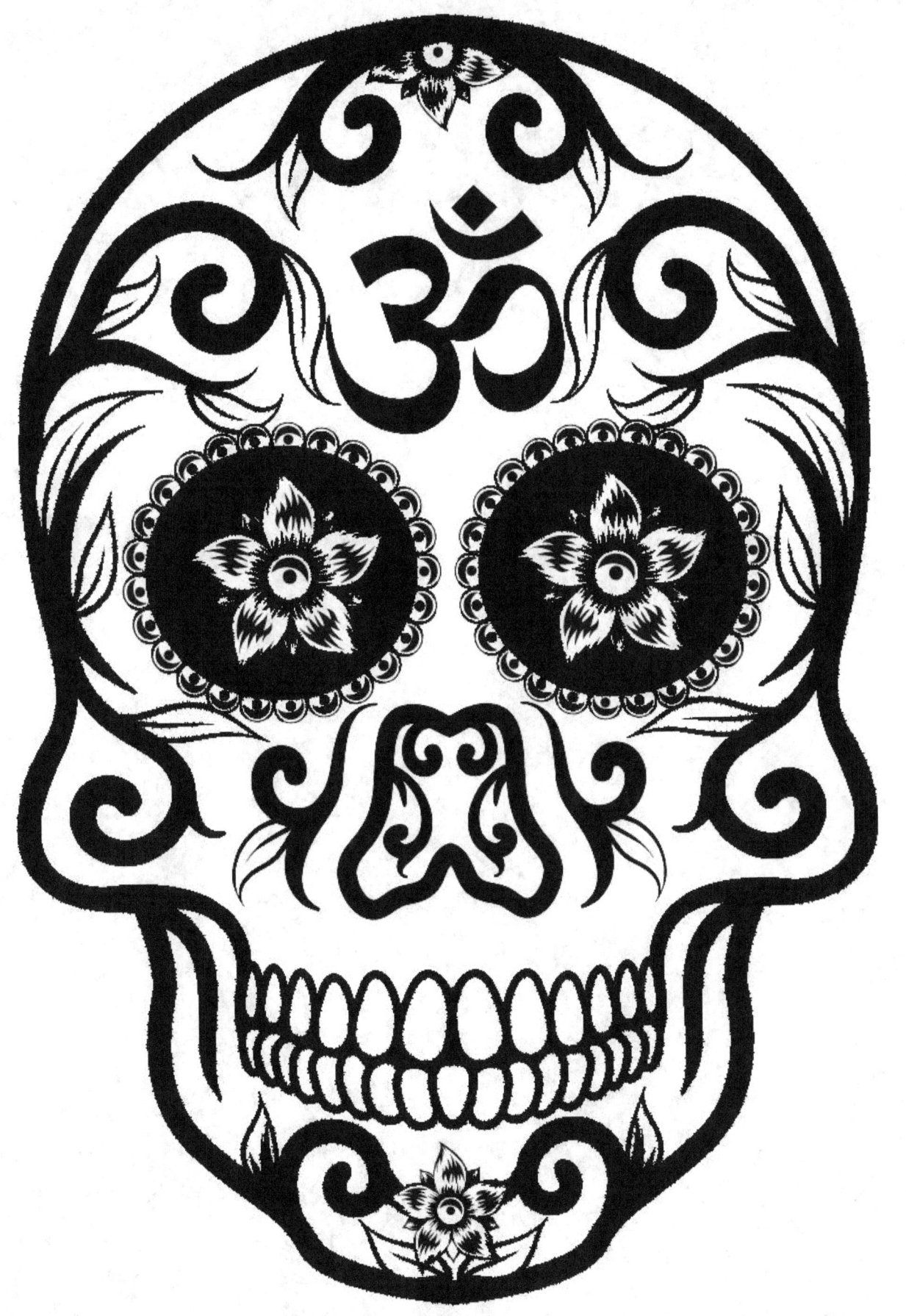

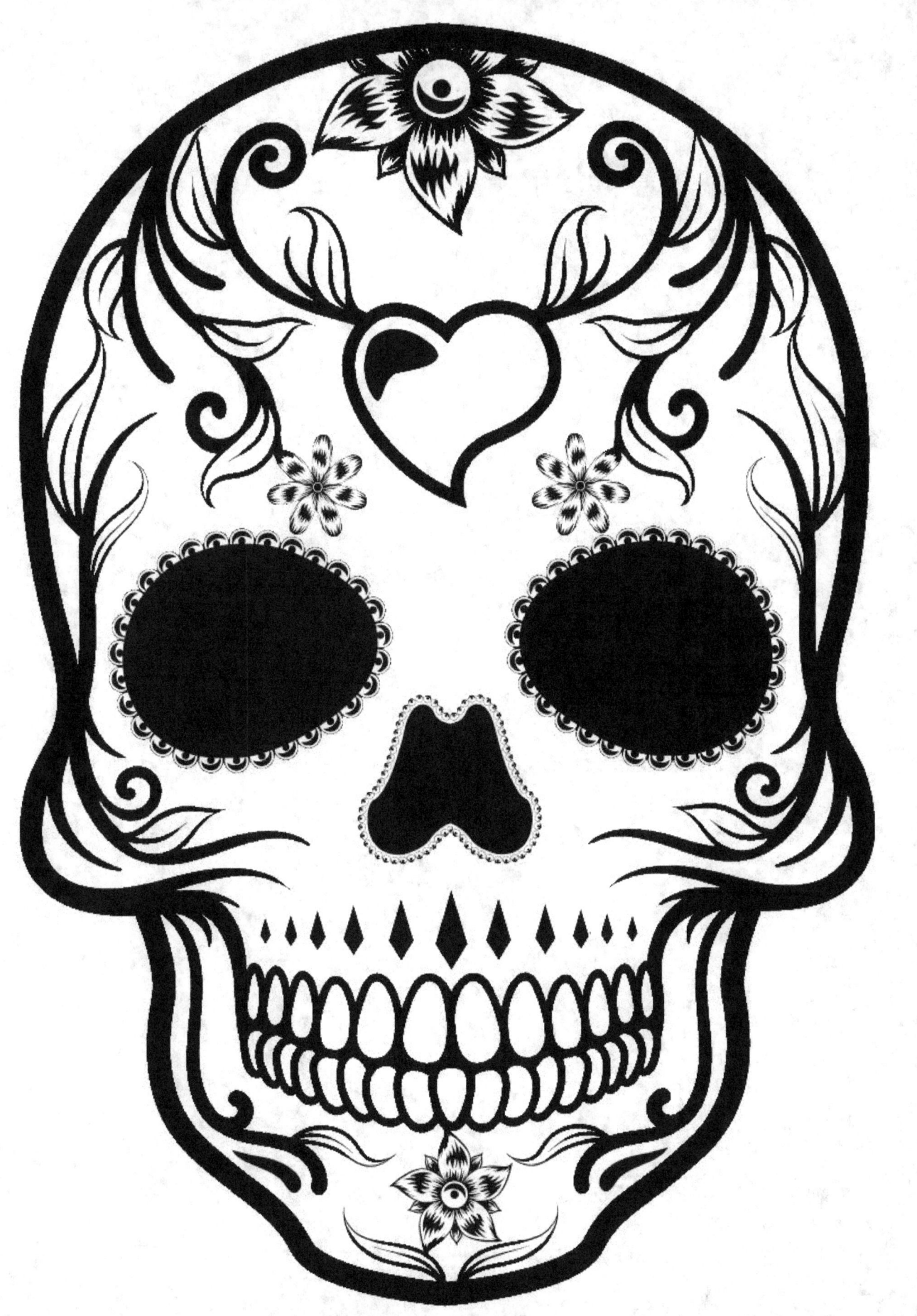

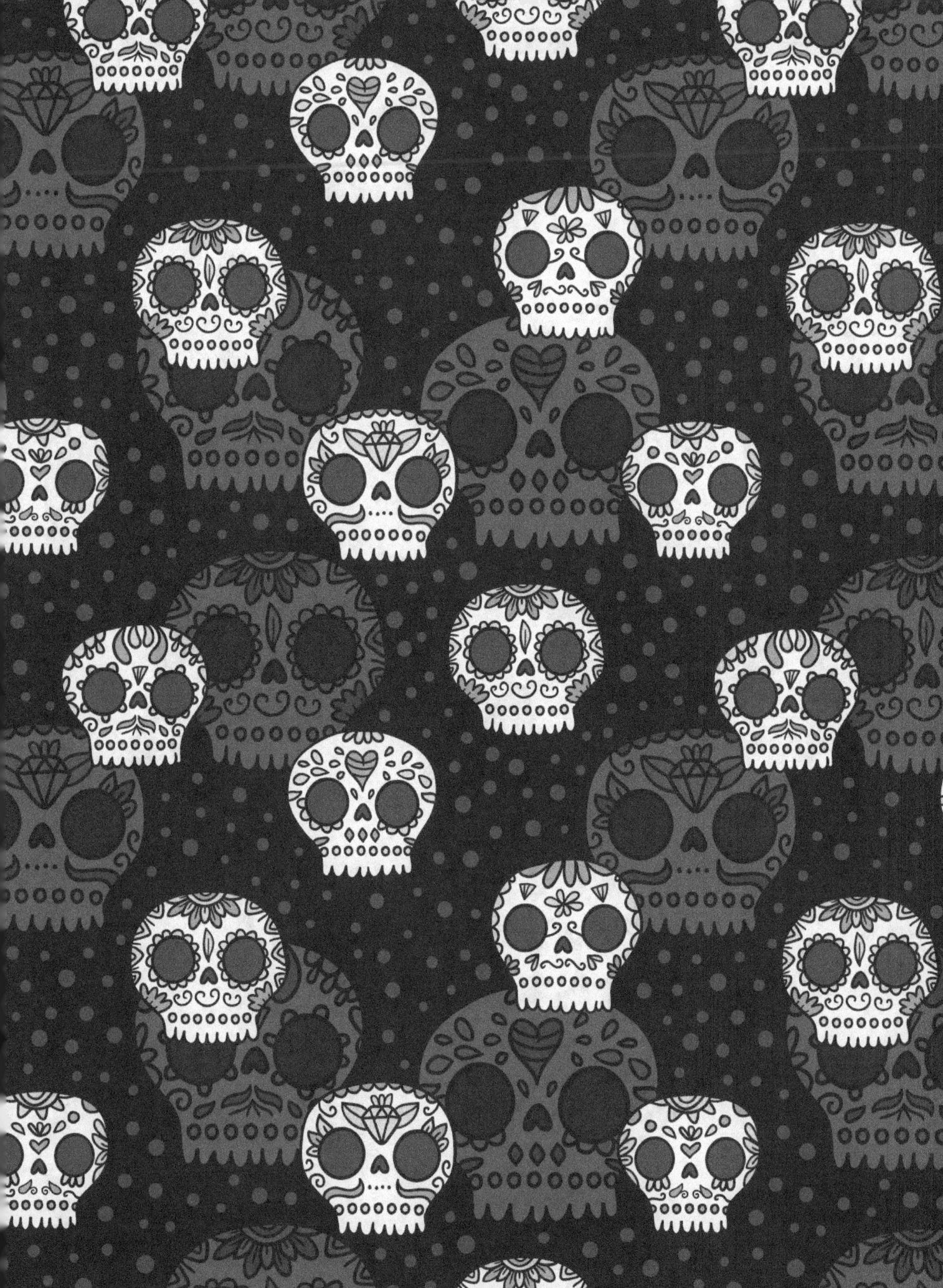

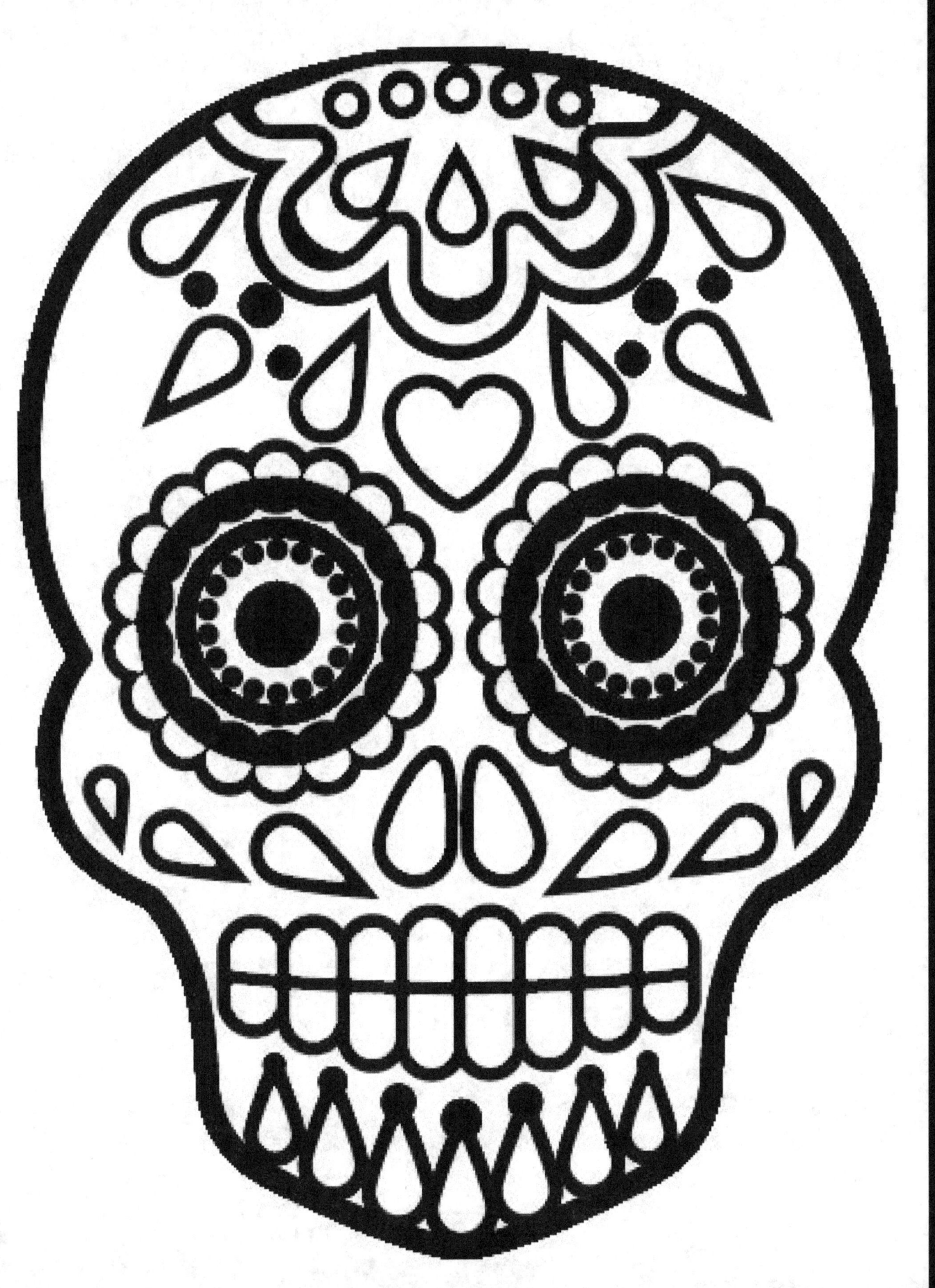

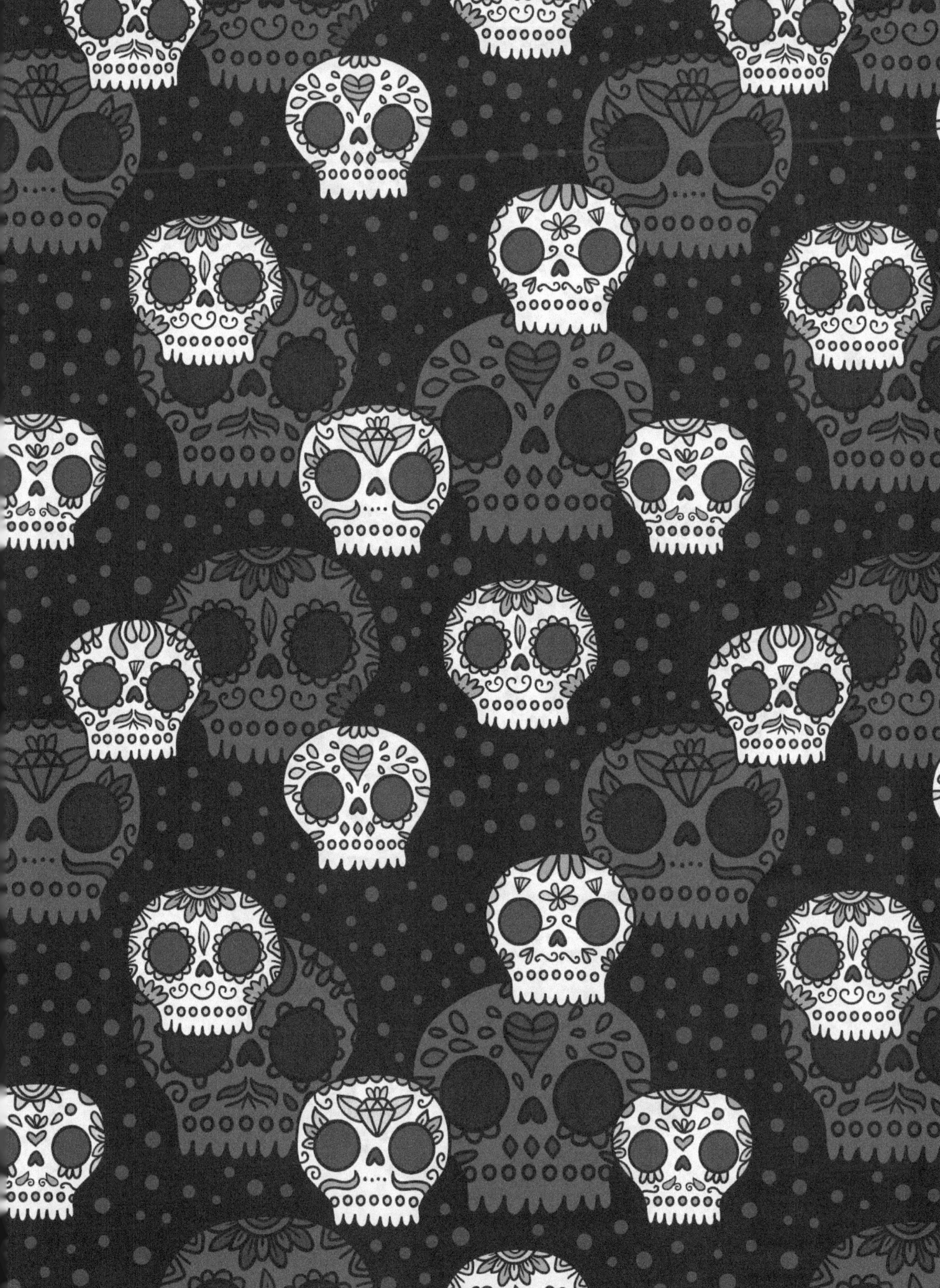

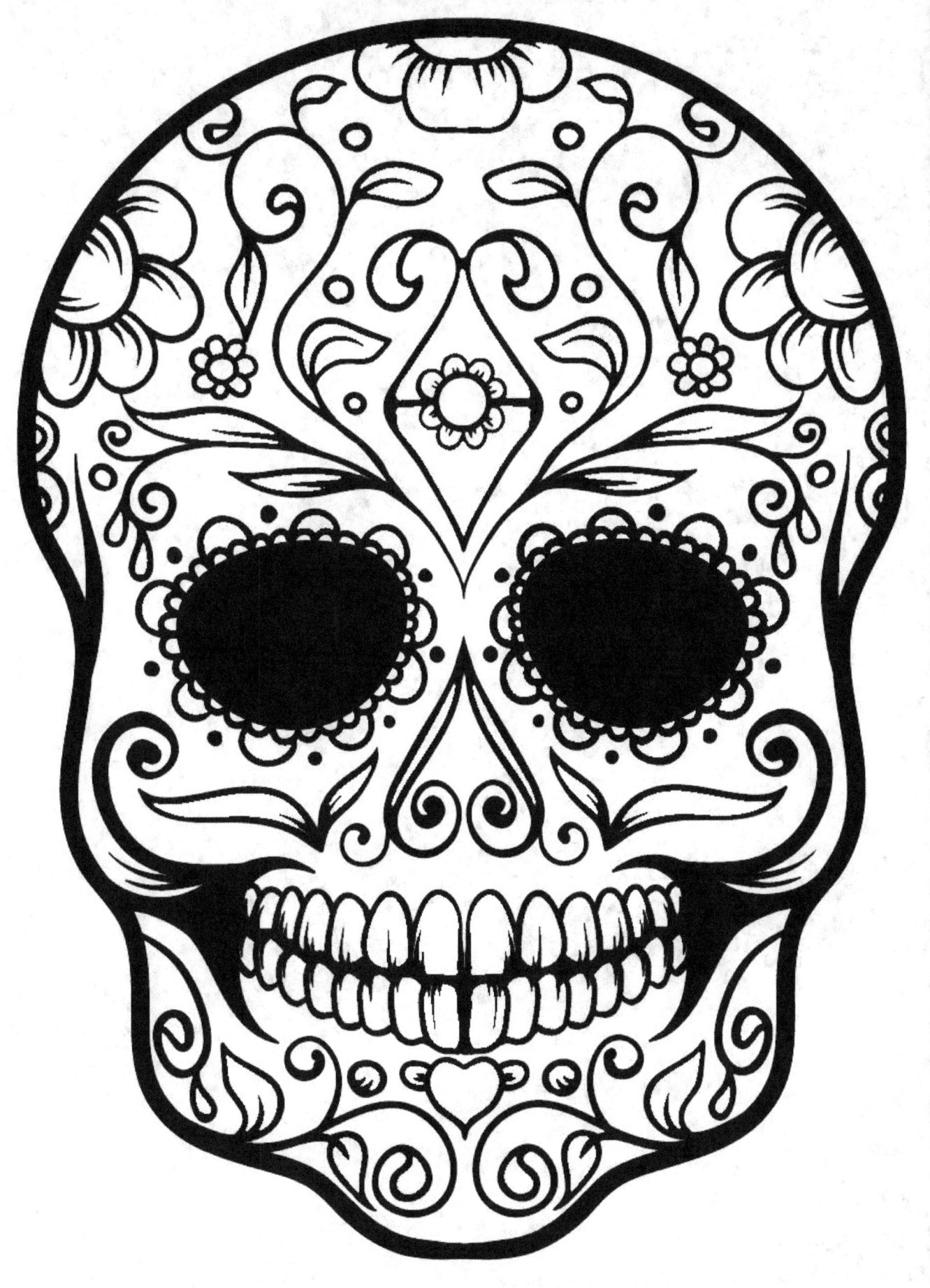

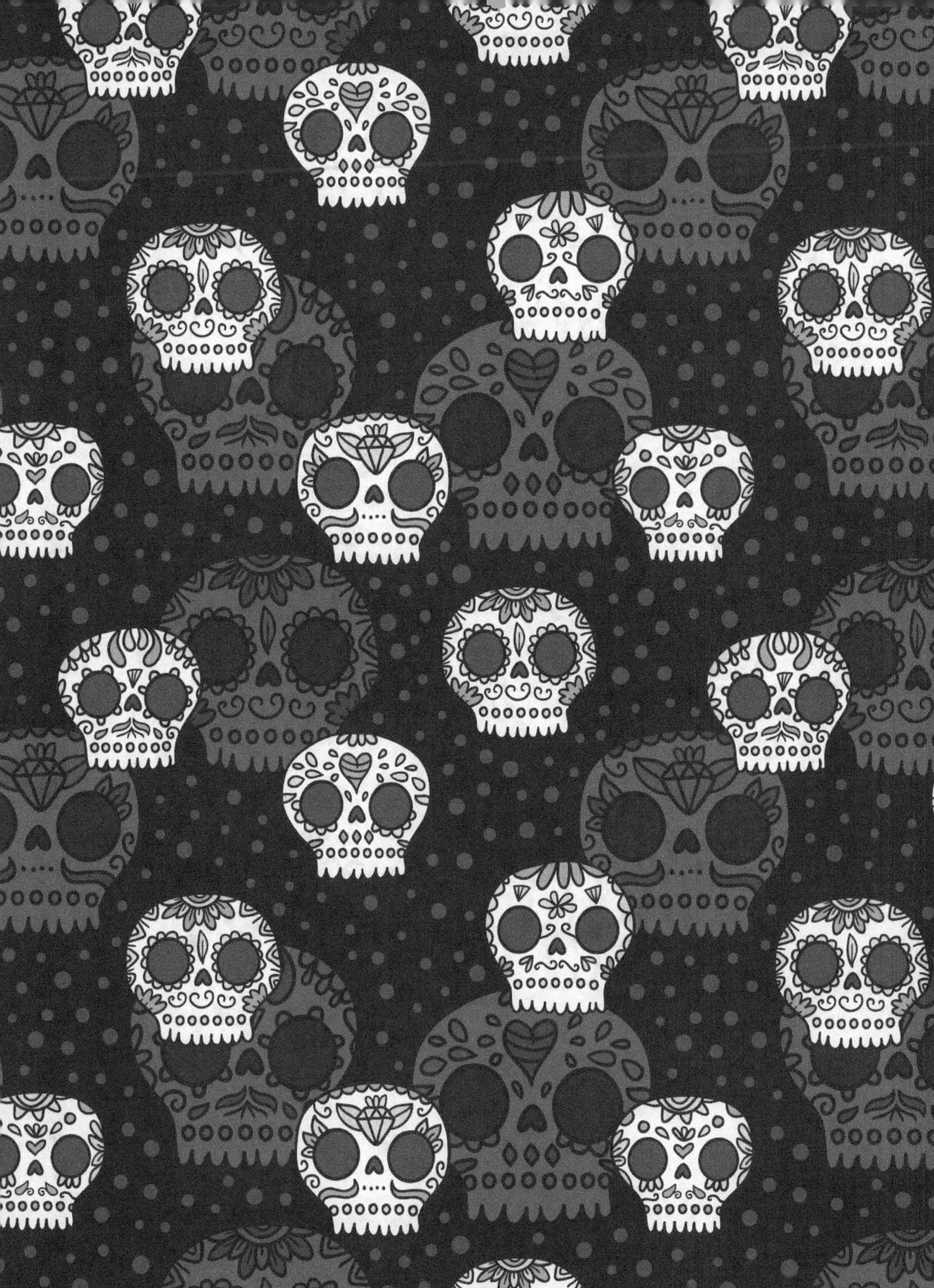

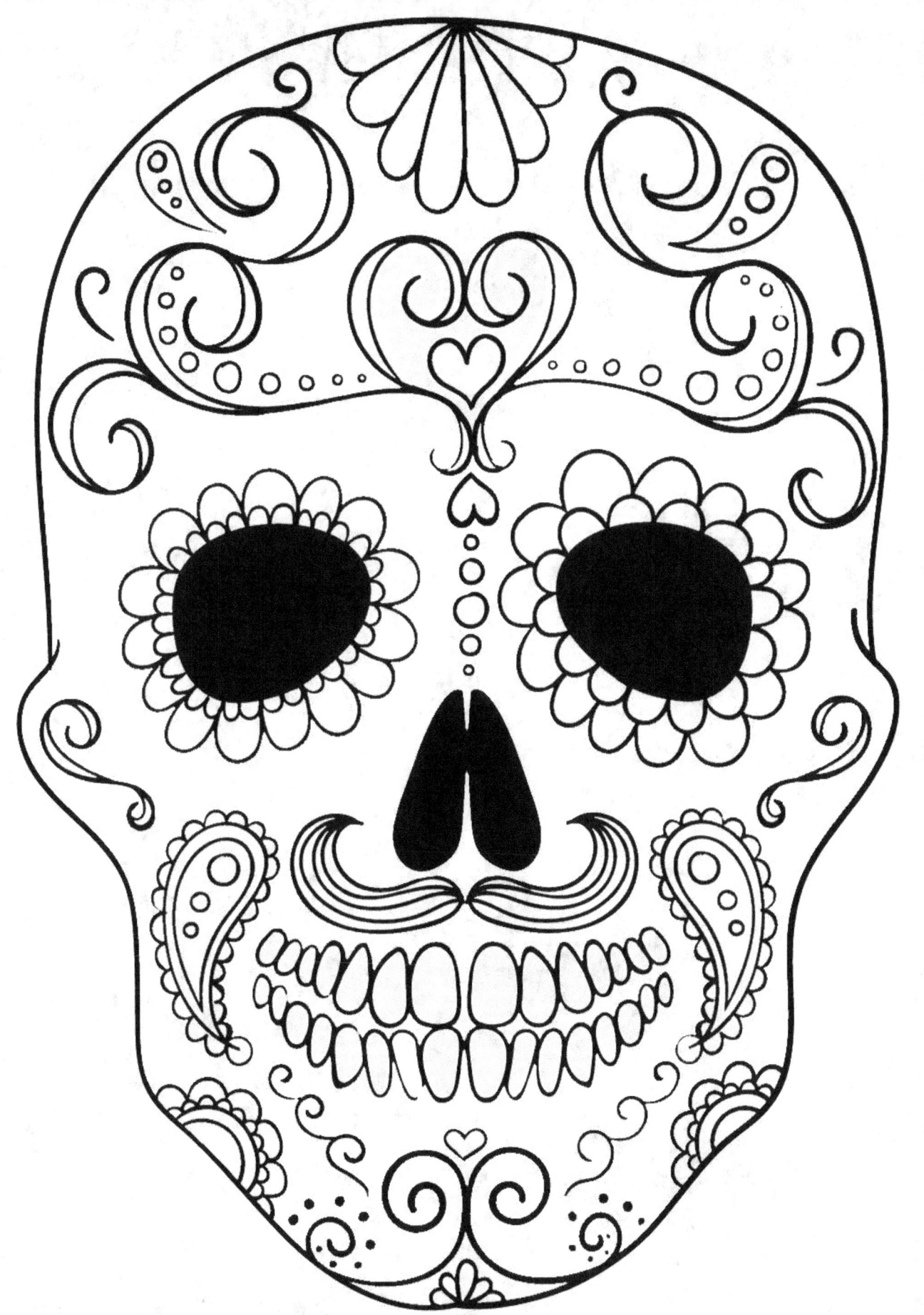

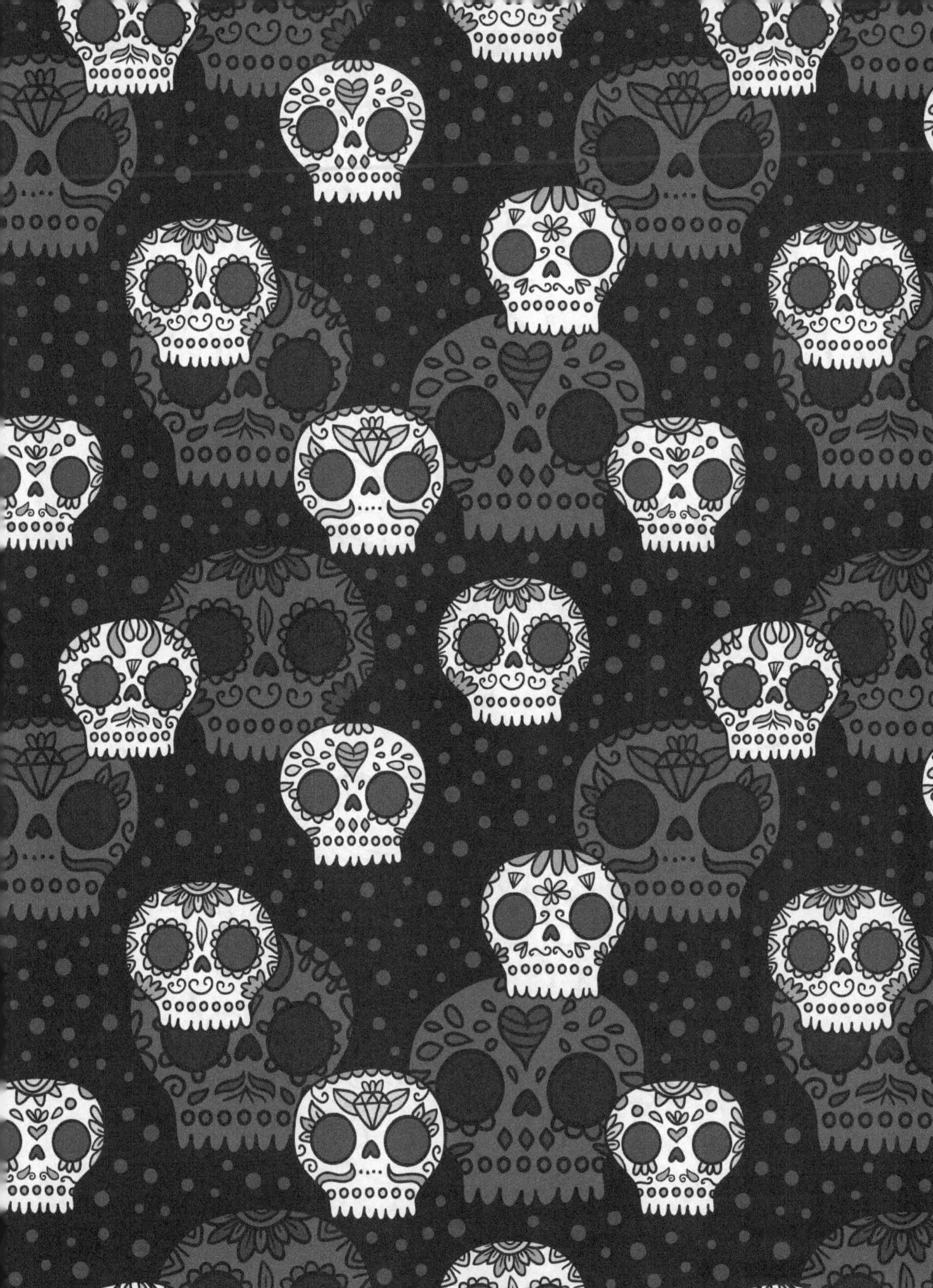

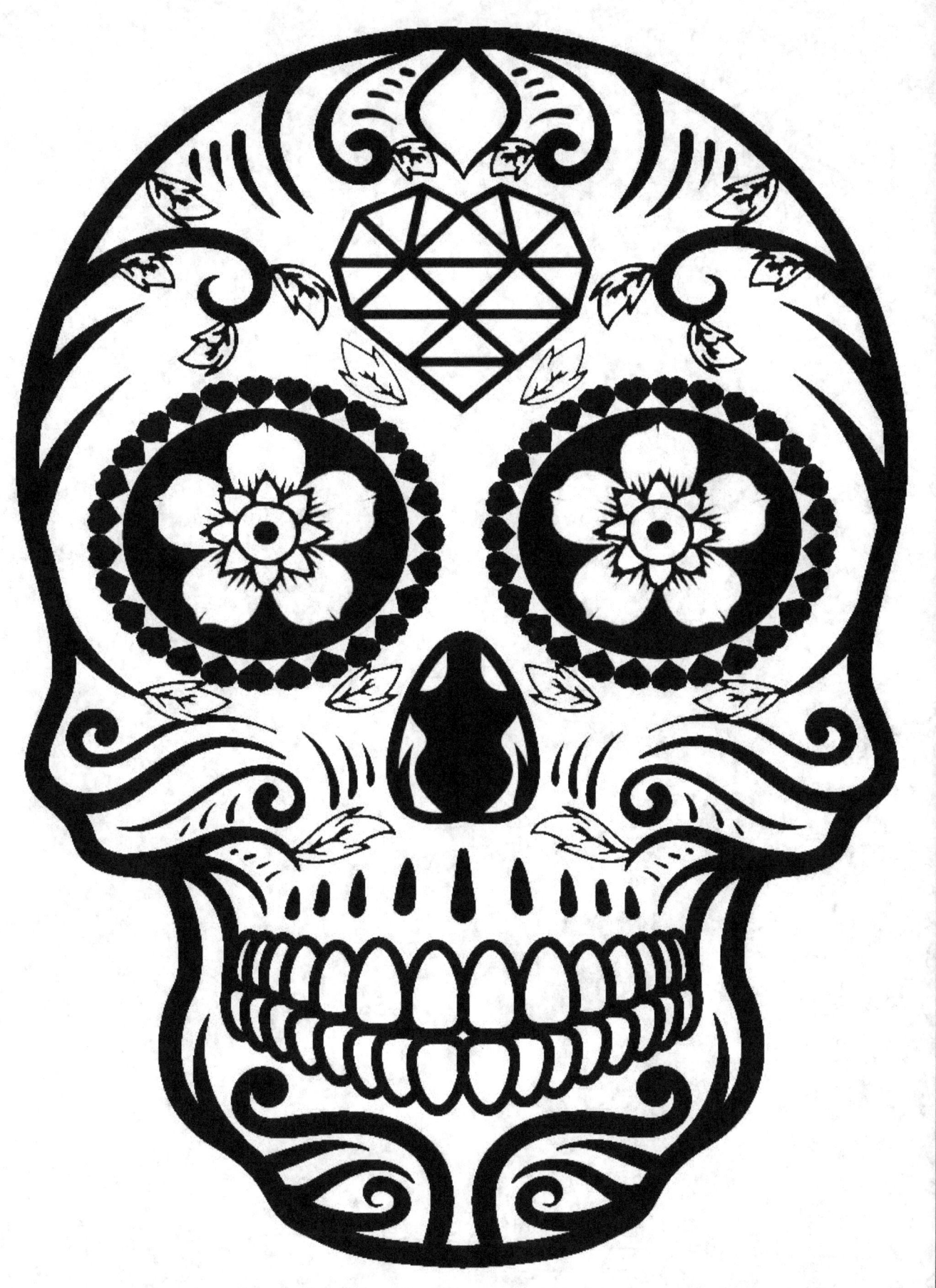

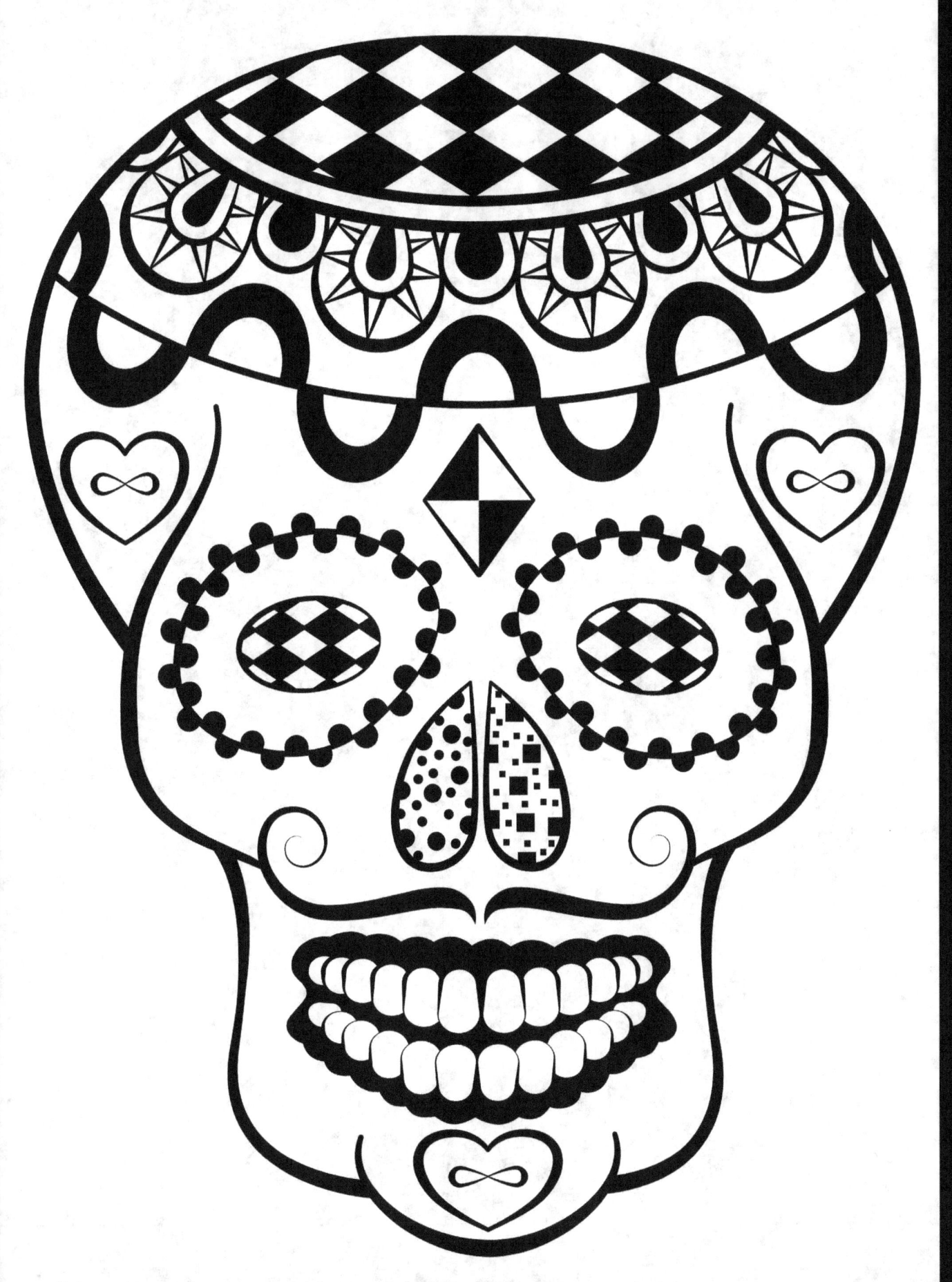

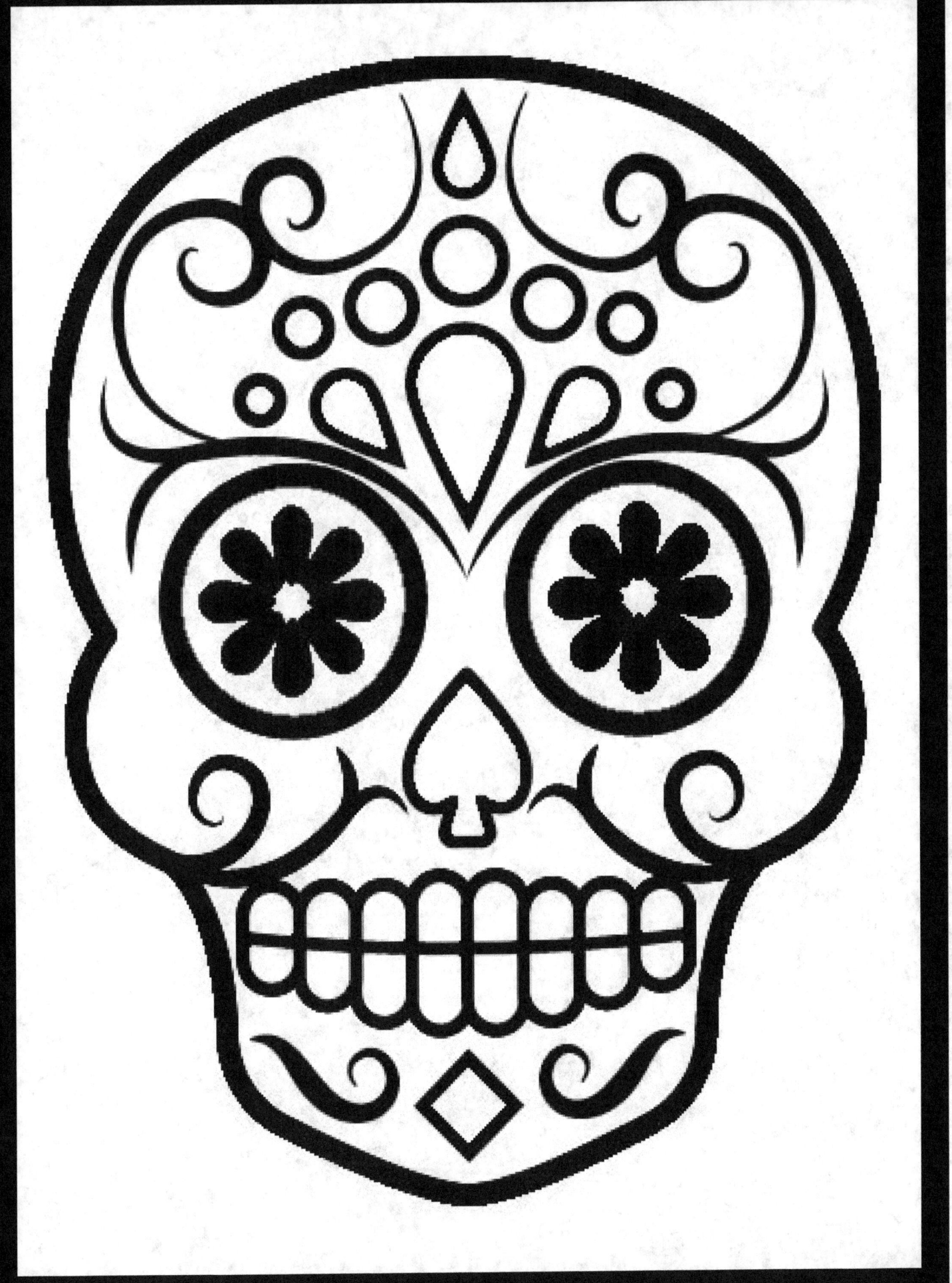

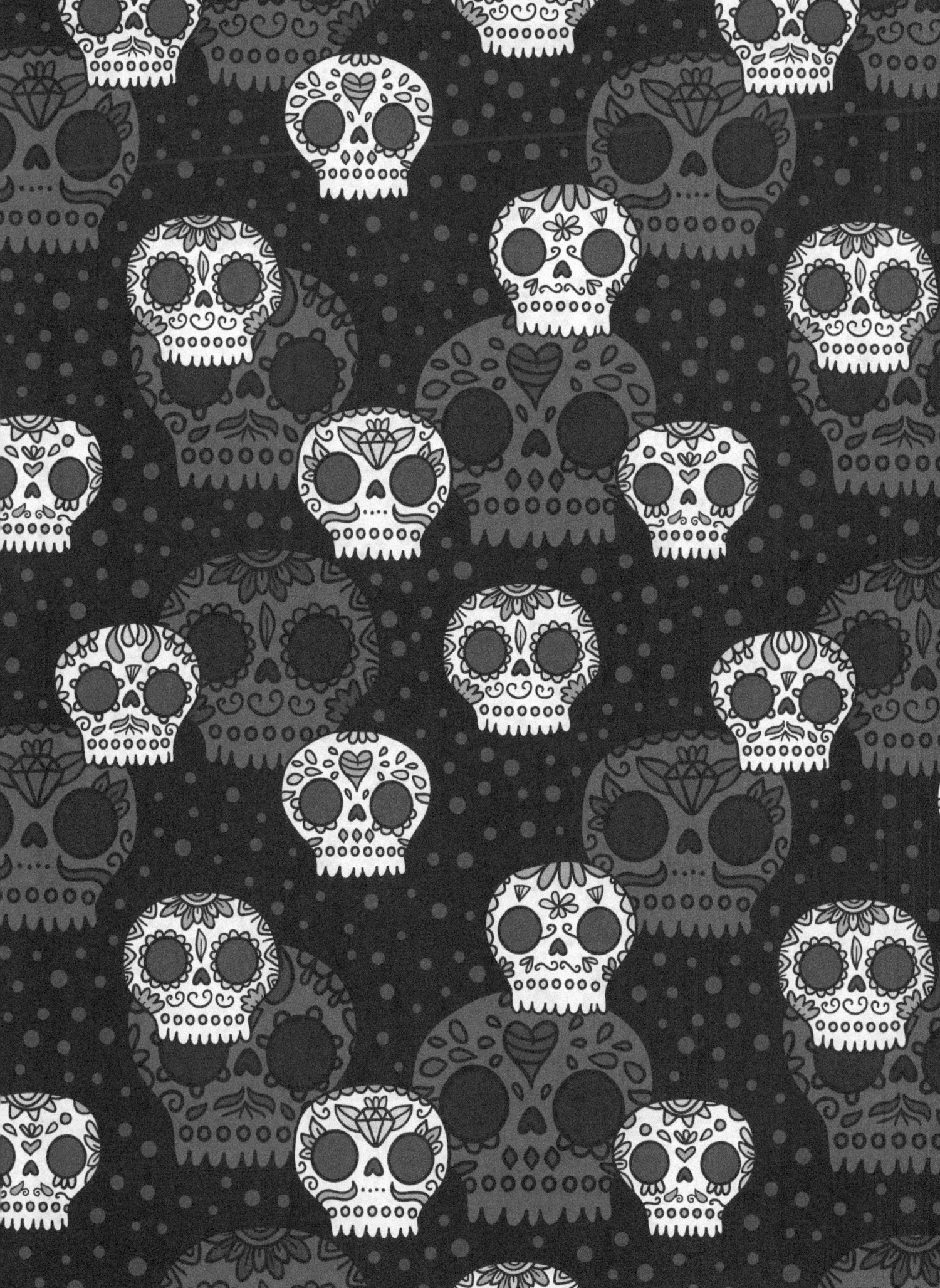

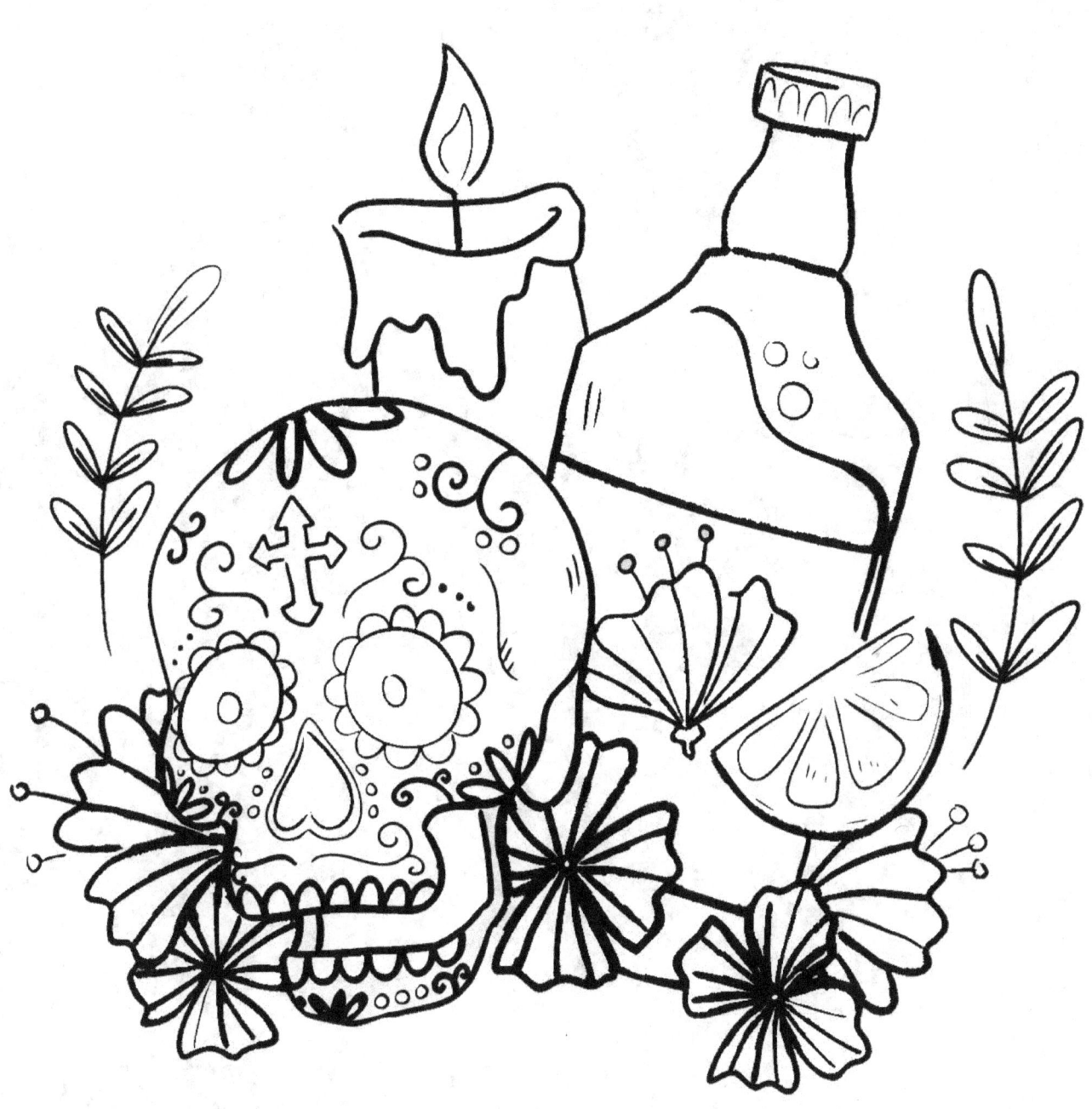

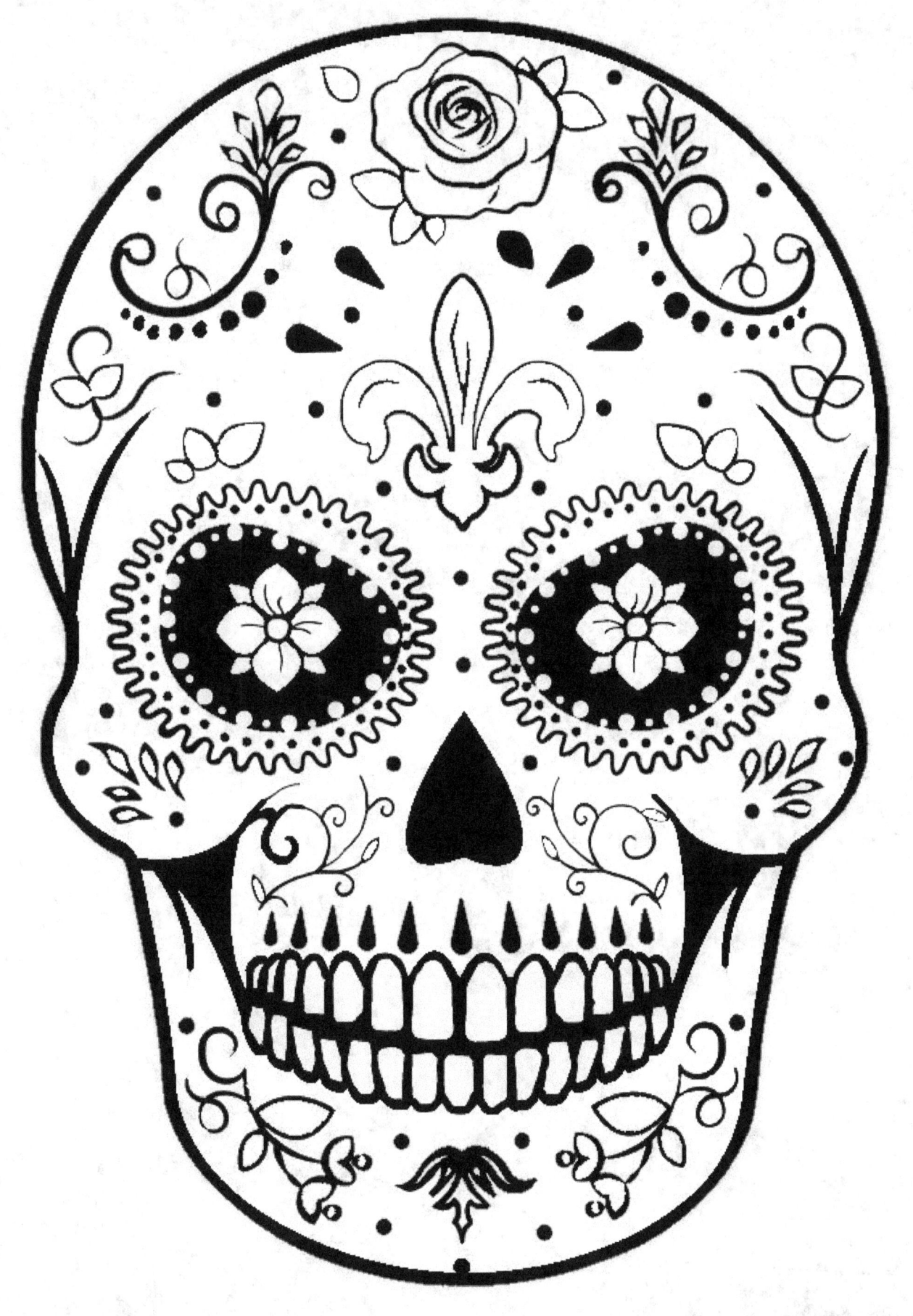

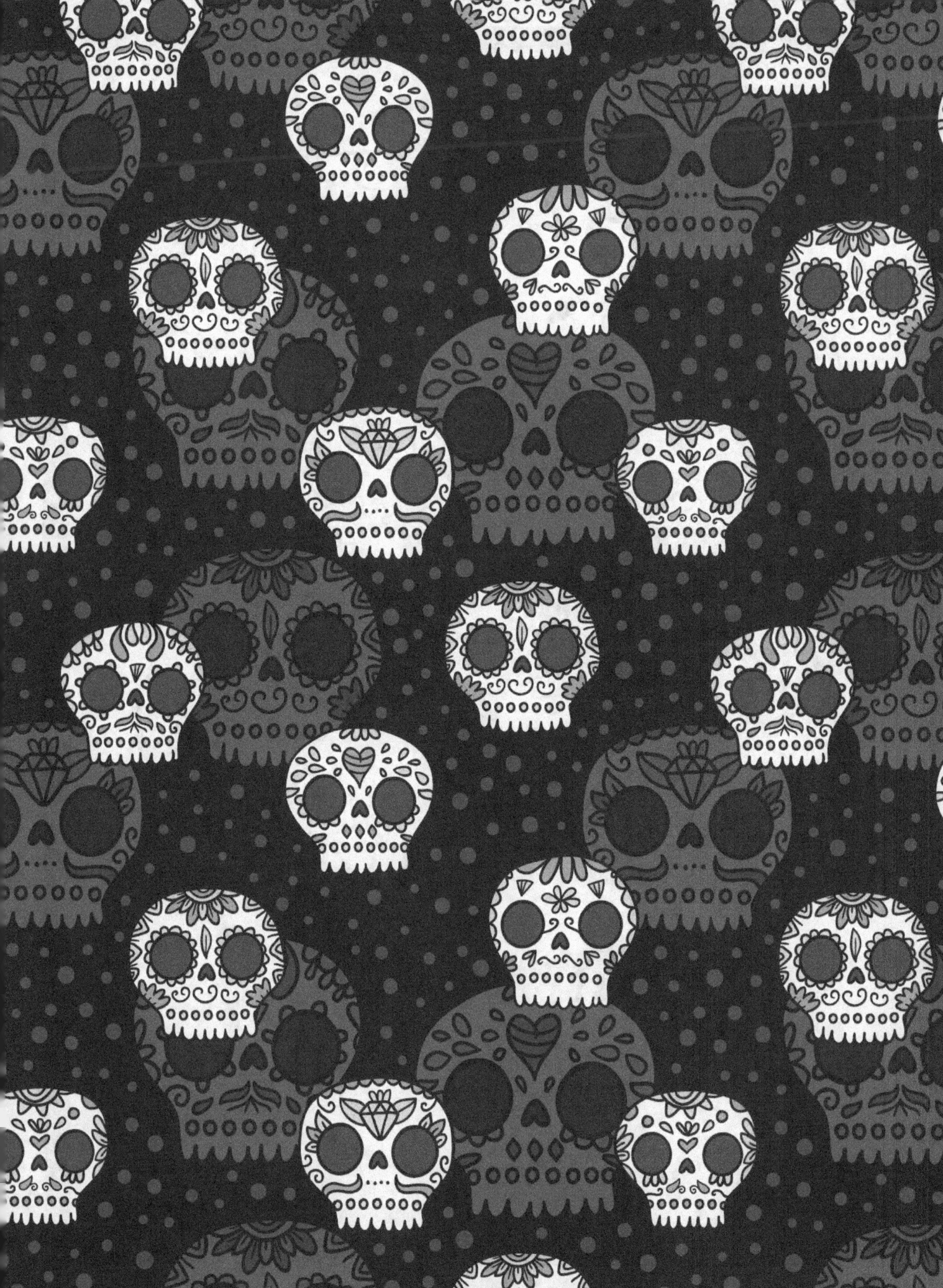

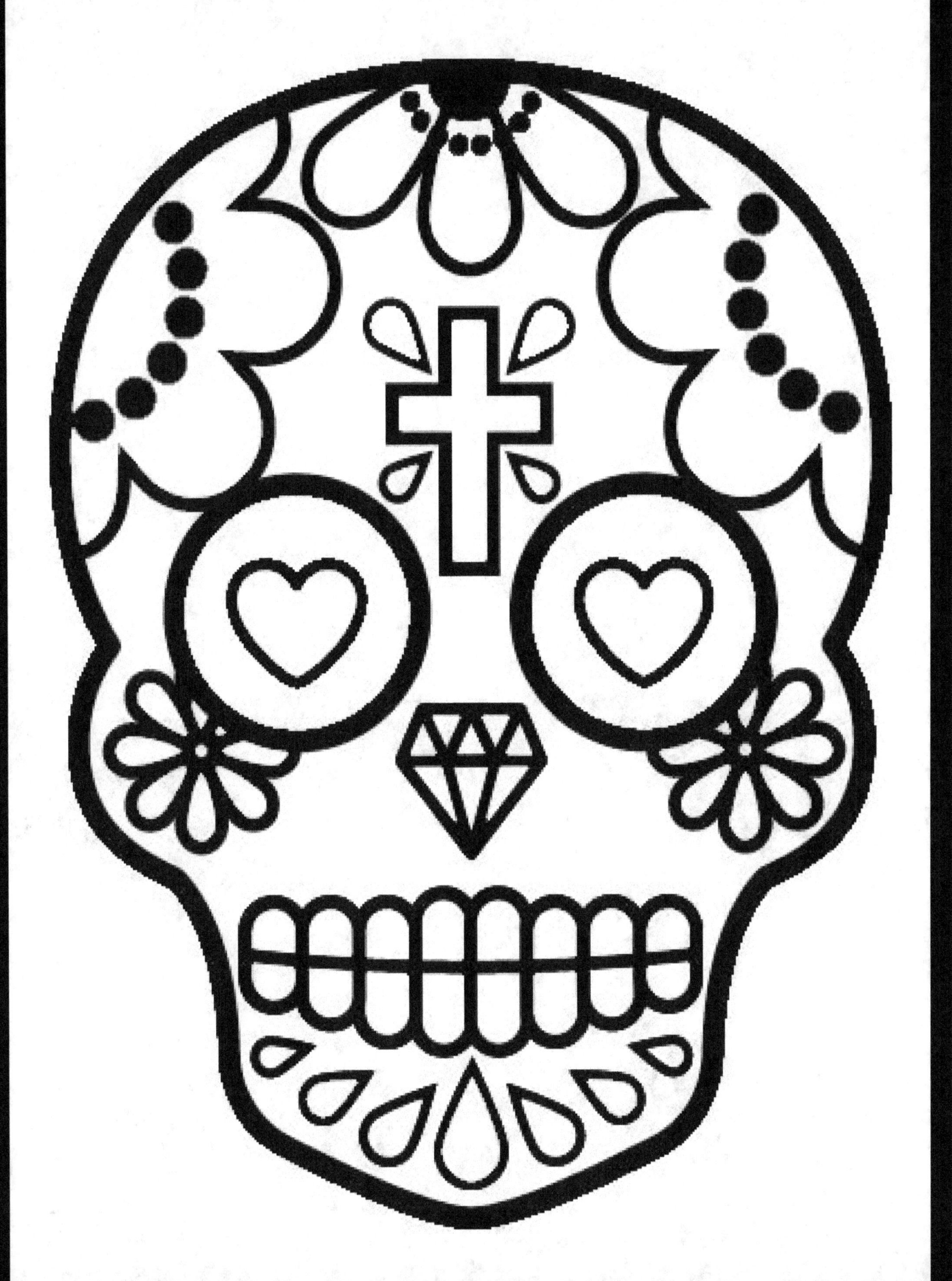

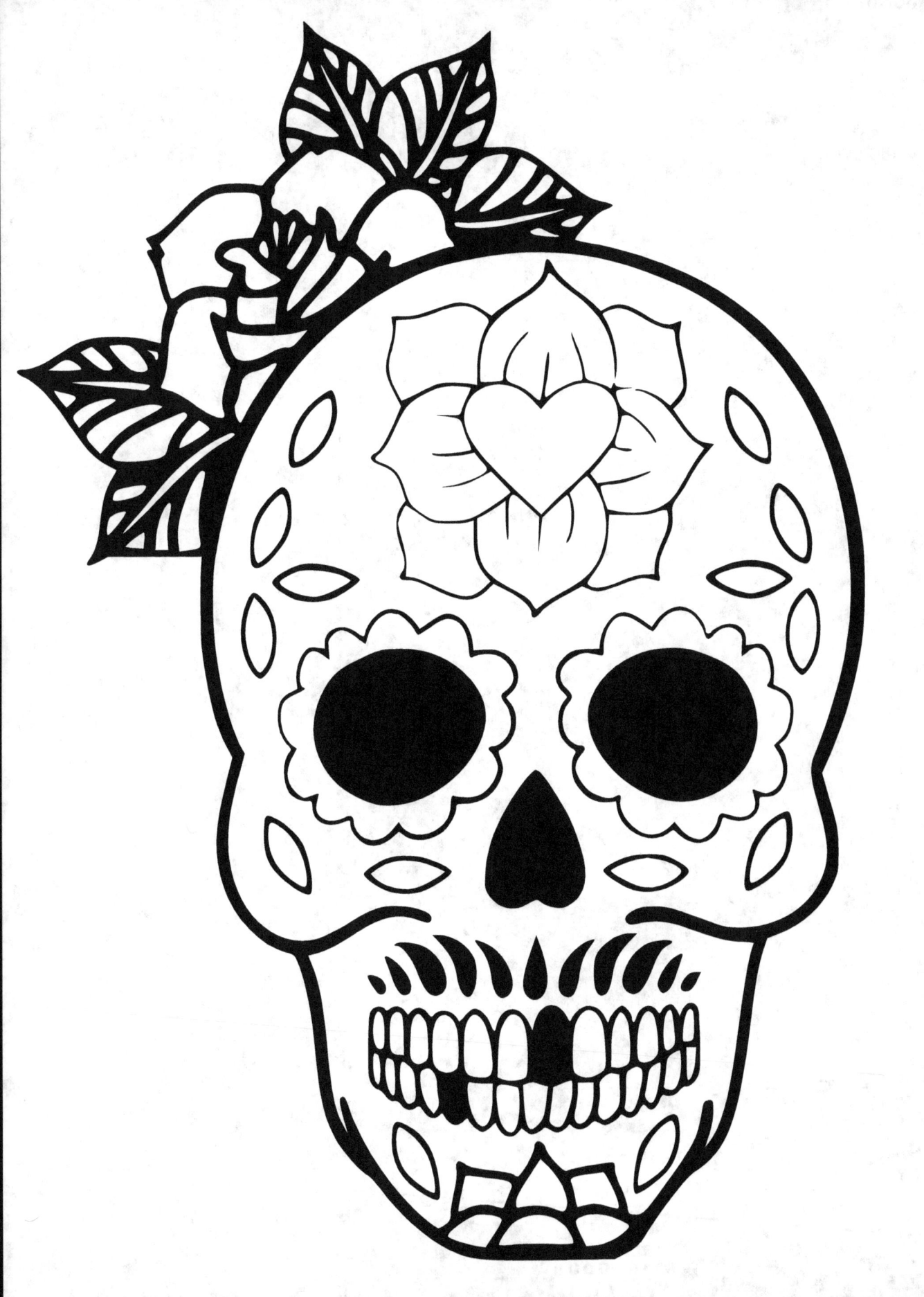

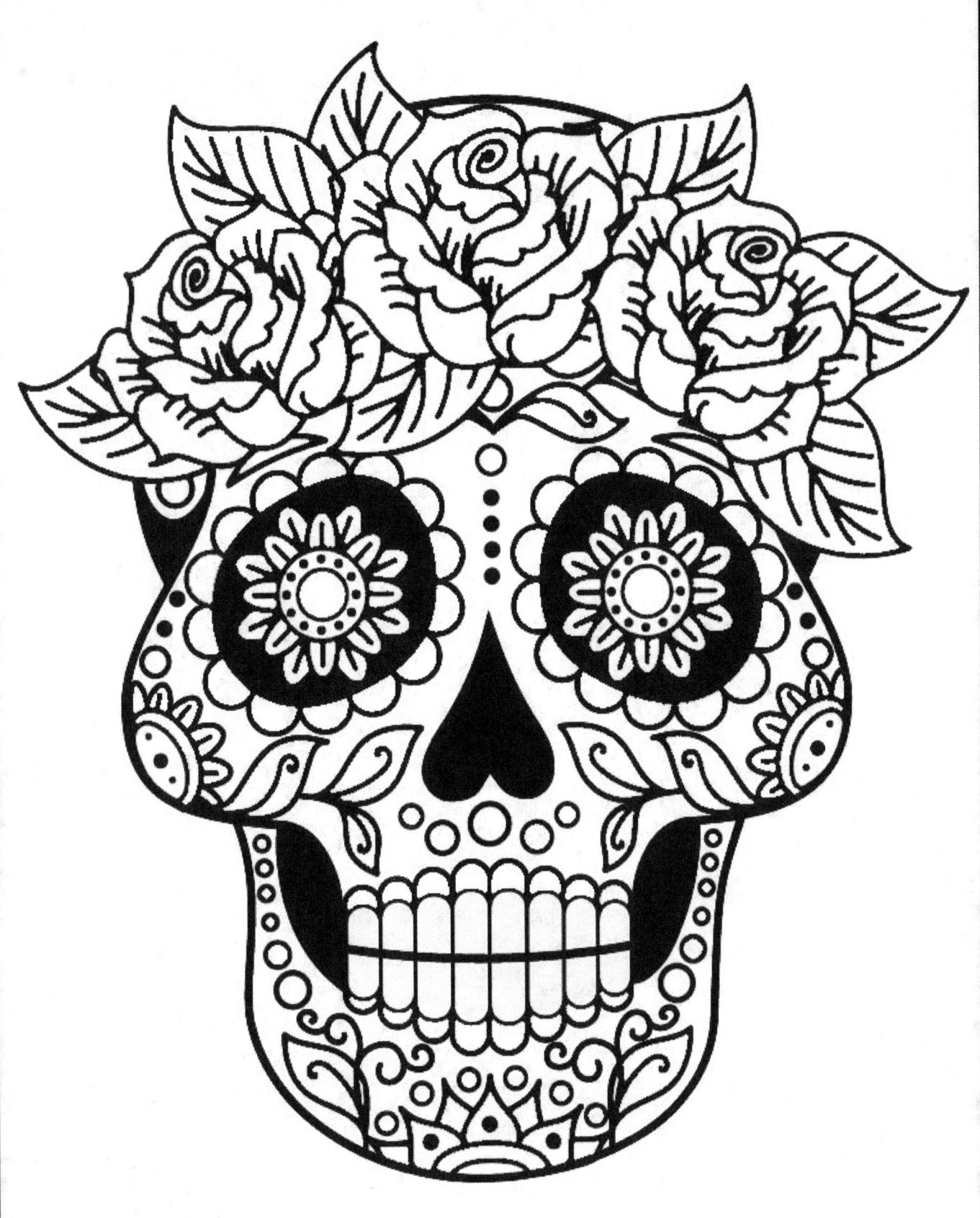

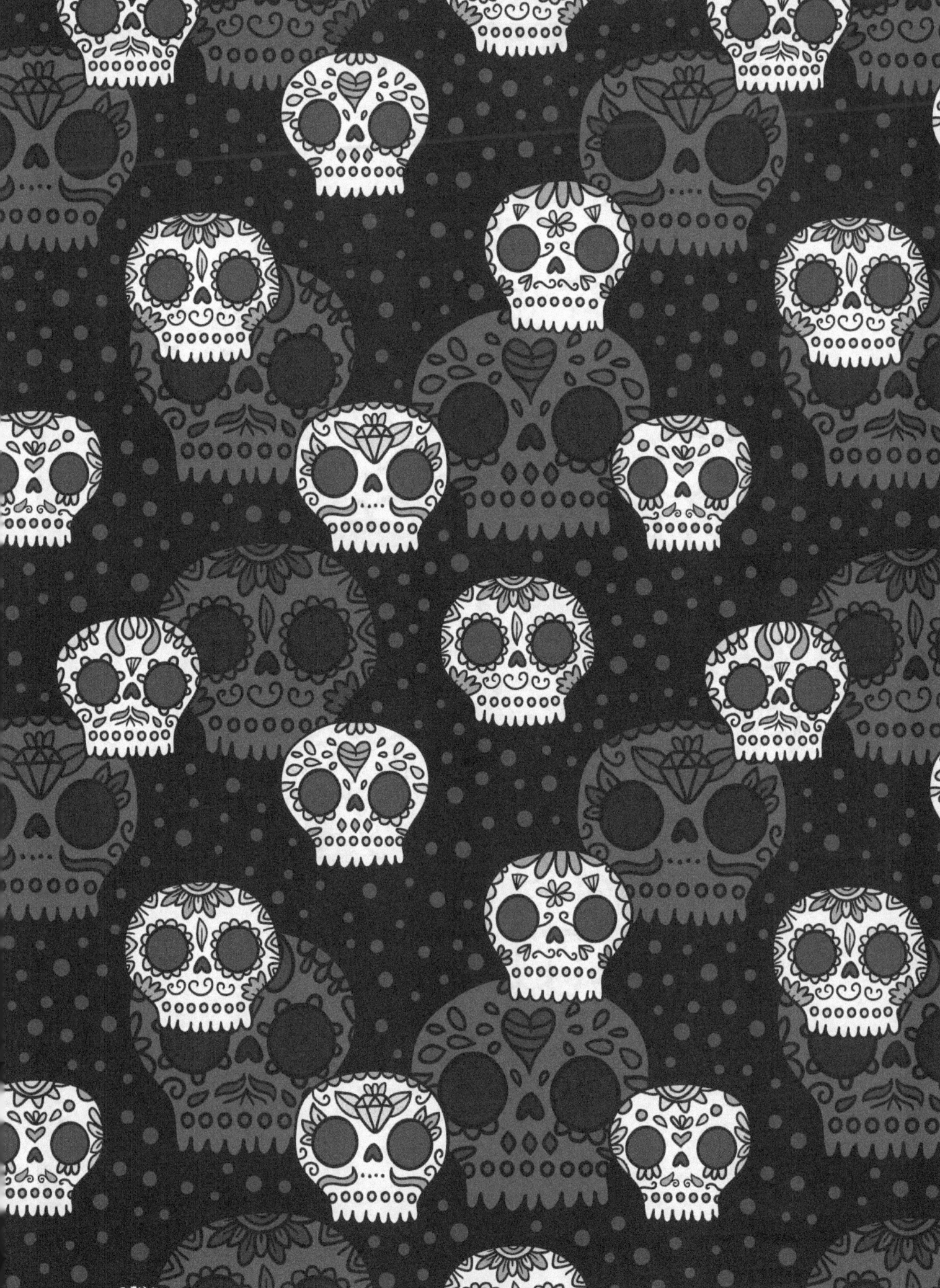

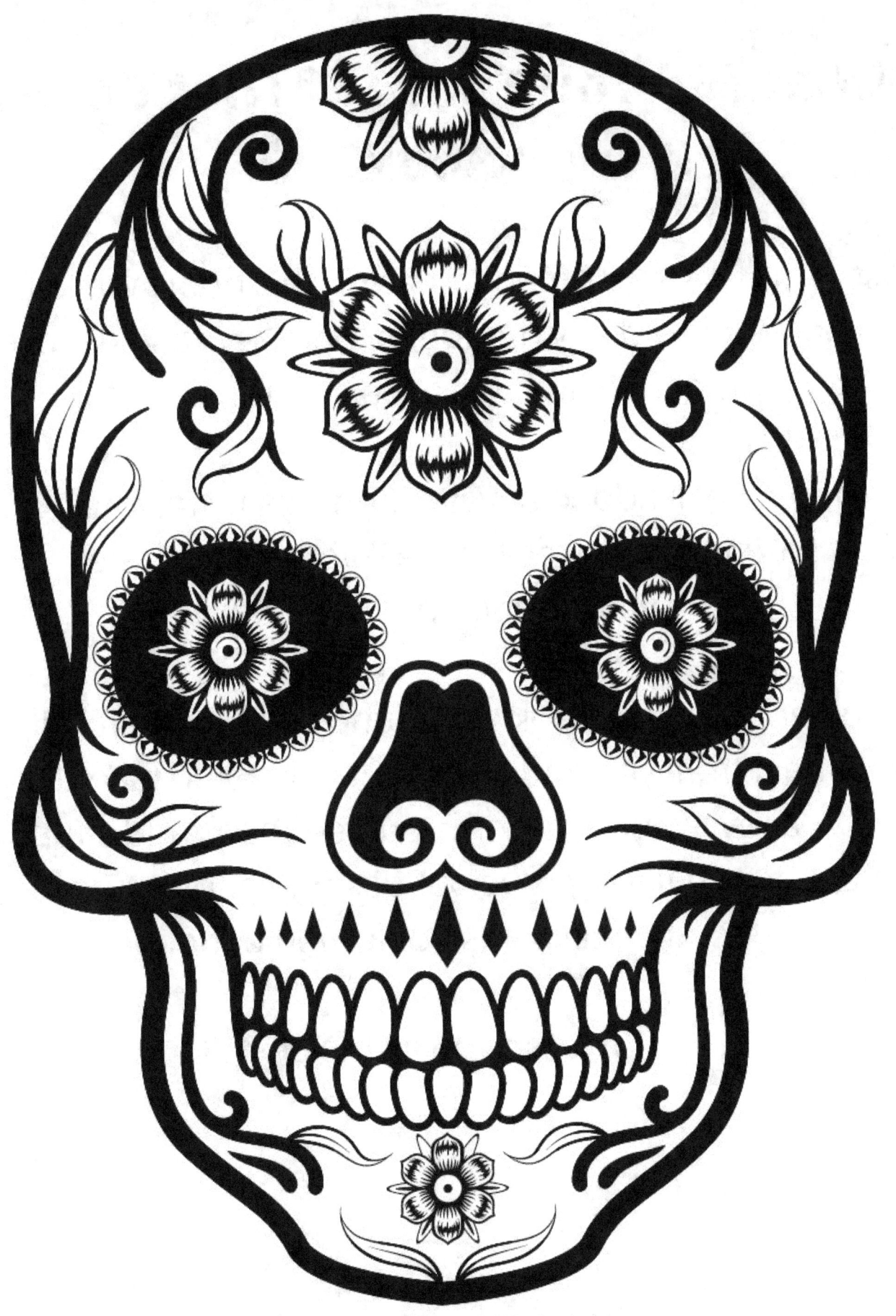

What Did You Think of That Coloring Book?

First of all, thank you for purchasing this book. We know you could have picked any number of books , but you picked this one and for that we are extremely grateful.

We hope that it added at value and quality to your everyday life. If so, it would be really nice if you could share this book with your friends and family.

If you enjoyed this book and found some benefit in it, we'd like to hear from you and hope that you could take some time to post a review on Amazon. Your feedback and support will help us to greatly improve our designing for future projects and make this book even better.

We wish you all the best !!!

Attributions to:
https://www.vecteezy.com
https://www.freepik.com

www.ingramcontent.com/pod-product-compliance
Lightning Source LLC
Chambersburg PA
CBHW080508220526
45465CB00006B/2413